healthy
VEGETARIAN & VEGAN
SLOW COOKER

healthy
VEGETARIAN & VEGAN
SLOW COOKER

**OVER 60 RECIPES FOR NUTRITIOUS, HOME-COOKED MEALS
FROM YOUR SLOW COOKER**

Nicola Graimes

Photography by Kate Whitaker

RYLAND PETERS & SMALL
LONDON • NEW YORK

Author and recipe developer Nicola Graimes

Senior designer Geoff Borin
Desk editor Emily Calder
Production manager Gordana Simakovic
Head of production Patricia Harrington
Creative director Leslie Harrington
Editorial director Julia Charles

Photographer Kate Whitaker
Prop stylist Kate Whitaker
Food stylist Bianca Nice
Proofreader Lisa Pendreigh
Indexer Vanessa Bird

Published in 2022
by Ryland Peters & Small
20–21 Jockey's Fields, London WC1R 4BW
and
341 E 116th St, New York NY 10029

www.rylandpeters.com

10 9 8 7 6 5 4 3 2 1

Text copyright © Nicola Graimes 2022
Design and photographs copyright
© Ryland Peters & Small 2022

ISBN: 978-1-78879-473-2
Printed in China

A CIP record for this book is available from the
British Library.
US Library of Congress Cataloging-in-Publication
Data has been applied for.

Notes
• All recipes in this book are made in a 3.5-litre/6-pint/
4-quart slow cooker.
• Both British (Metric) and American (Imperial plus
US cups) measurements are included in these recipes
for your convenience, however it is important to
work with one set of measurements and not alternate
between the two within a recipe.
• All spoon measurements are level unless otherwise
specified: 1 tablespoon is 15 ml; 1 teaspoon is 5 ml.
• Not all cheeses are vegetarian as they may include
animal rennet. When buying cheese, it's a good idea
to check they are produced using vegetarian rennet.
• Whenever butter is called for within these recipes,
unsalted butter (or a dairy-free equivalent for vegans)
should be used.
• Citrus fruit is commonly waxed with shellac or
beeswax, neither of which are suitable for vegans.
When a recipe calls for the grated zest of citrus,
buy unwaxed fruit and wash well before using.
• Uncooked or partially cooked eggs should not be
served to the very old, frail, young children, pregnant
women or those with compromised immune systems.

Disclaimer
The views expressed in this book are those of the
author but they are general views only and readers are
urged to consult a relevant and qualified specialist or
physician for individual advice before beginning any
dietary regimen. Ryland Peters & Small hereby exclude
all liability to the extent permitted by law for any errors
or omissions in this book and for any loss, damage or
expense (whether direct or indirect) suffered by a third
party relying on any information and instruction
contained in this book. You should always consult
your physician before changing your dietary regimen.

CONTENTS

INTRODUCTION

For me, slow cookers are a much-underrated asset in the kitchen. If you have one tucked in the nether regions of a cupboard, it's now time to get it out, wipe it down and use it. The slow cooker has so many attributes, notably it's easy to use, economical and energy-friendly to run and let's not forget there's something quite special about a slow-cooked dish. It's almost an antidote to hectic, modern life and the preoccupation with quick meals and fast food.

Testing and writing these recipes felt almost meditative and therapeutic, especially since it came at a particularly stressful time of my life. The beauty of using a slow cooker is its simplicity, I like the idea that you largely bung a handful of ingredients into the pot, turn it on and leave the cooker to do its thing. In keeping, I've tried to maintain this simplicity with the recipes in this book, using readily available, nutritious, fresh ingredients and cooking them in a simple, unfussy, economic way. There are some concessions to this, including frying an onion or toasting spices at the beginning of a recipe, as I've found in most places this makes a difference to the final flavour of the dish.

When some consider slow cookers, rich, meaty, wintery stews may spring to mind, but they are much more versatile than they are perhaps given credit for. Think mushroom dumplings in a light broth, fresh fruit jam, a nutmeg-infused brown rice pudding, a chestnut, cashew and herb loaf or a Korean braised tofu pot – just a handful of the recipes in this book. In the meat-free kitchen, the slow cooker is perfect for cooking inexpensive staples such as beans, lentils and grains.

Simple, everyday fresh ingredients have the power to support and boost our health but, for me, it's more than just about physical wellbeing – healthy ingredients can be as good for the soul as they are for the body. Just consider a tasty, nutritious bowl of filling squash soup made with a nurturing ginger-infused broth and lots of veg – it ticks all the right boxes.

Slow cookers cook food gently and evenly and it is arguable that the lower cooking temperature may help to preserve nutrients that can be lost when food is cooked quickly at a high heat, such as frying, grilling/broiling and boiling. Additionally, since the food is contained within a covered pot, nutrients released from the food could be contained in the slow cooker within any liquid or sauce; although, fat-soluble vitamins (A, D, E and K) tend to hold up better than water-soluble ones such as vitamins B and C.

Cooking foods slowly at a lower temperature is also less likely to expose us to advanced glycation end products (AGEs), which are toxins created by grilling/broiling and frying foods at high temperatures, especially animal products. AGEs have been linked to Alzheimer's disease, inflammation, diabetes, vascular and kidney disease as well as ageing skin.

To enable you to eat good healthy food at any time of the day, the recipes in this book cover most type of meal, from breakfast and brunch to weekday meals and dishes more suited to weekend cooking. Some dishes may require a little forward planning, but pretty much all the hard work is done by the slow cooker. The recipes are organised by type of dish, so you'll discover soups and broths, curries, stews and one-pot dishes, large veg dishes as well as those that could be served as part of a mezze platter or side dish. In the main they are savoury, with a few fruity dishes for breakfast.

I have purposefully chosen dishes that I believe work best in a slow cooker in terms of taste and simplicity – there is little point choosing an ingredient or dish that cooks in 10 minutes on the hob/stovetop to then spend hours cooking it in a slow cooker if the latter adds nothing in terms of flavour and convenience. The true beauty of a slow cooker is that dishes pretty much look after themselves – there's no need to hover over the hob/stovetop to produce nutritious, economical, tasty meals.

AN ECONOMICAL WAY TO COOK

One of the key advantages of using a slow cooker, particularly relevant today, is how economical and how energy efficient it is – what's more, the initial outlay is much less than if you were to buy a new oven. Cheaper to run than an oven and using less electricity than a conventional light bulb, your average slow cooker typically uses between 75–150 watts of electricity per hour on low and between 150–210 watts of electricity on high. A hob/stovetop uses between 1,000–2,000 watts of power per hour – cooking for 8 hours in a slow cooker uses a similar amount of energy a hob/stovetop uses in just 45 minutes – while an oven uses around 2,000–2,300 watts per hour over a medium-high heat. Modern slow cookers are said to be one of the most energy-efficient appliances in the kitchen.

ABOUT THE RECIPES

All the recipes in this book have been tested in a 3.5-litre/6-pint/4-quart slow cooker and mainly feed four people. Only the high and low settings were used as these are standard on all models and the slow cooker was not preheated.

The slow cooker used for testing had a lightweight metal, non-stick coated pot that can be used on the hob/stovetop for pre-browning. It tends to cook more quickly than a slow cooker with a heavier ceramic pot so please bear this in mind when cooking the recipes. Each recipe comes with a range of cooking times – the shorter time tells you that the food will be tender and ready to eat but will not deteriorate if left to cook for the longer time given. It also allows for differences in performance between the many models of slow cooker available.

CHOOSING A SLOW COOKER

Slow cookers come in many variations with features and prices to suit all needs. If you are thinking of buying a slow cooker there are a few things to consider.

WHAT SIZE?

Generally speaking, slow cookers are available in three basic sizes – small, medium and large and may be oval or round in shape. The working capacity is usually slightly less than stated on the packaging as you must not fill the slow cooker right to the brim – at least half full is the ideal.

ROUND OR OVAL?

Round slow cookers are a good choice if you are going to cook mainly soups and stew-type recipes. An oval pot is a little more versatile and is an ideal shape if making nut roasts, or similar, in a loaf tin.

FEATURES

Removable inner pots These are made from stoneware, ceramic or lightweight non-stick coated metal. Stoneware and ceramic pots are heavier to lift and cannot be used on the hob/stovetop but look great taken to the table for serving. Metal pots can be used directly on the hob/stovetop for pre-browning and searing foods – the pot is then placed in the base unit – so it's much quicker and more convenient. These pots are lighter to lift, too, so it's easier to pour and serve or turn out foods. Metal pots may cook a little faster than those made from stoneware and ceramic so cooking times may be shorter in these models. Always check the manufacturer's instructions.

Transparent lids A clear toughened glass or heavy-duty plastic lid will allow you to keep an eye on the food as it's cooking.

Digital controls Some models have digital controls that enable you to set the cooking time on the unit. It will count down and automatically switch to 'keep warm'. This is useful if you don't want to use a separate timer.

SETTINGS

Slow cookers reach just below boiling point 100°C/212°F during cooking – this temperature is reached more quickly on the high setting. All models vary slightly in performance – some cook more quickly than others. You will soon get used to your own model.

Basic cookers just have low and high settings and an 'off' position. Some may also have a medium, auto or warm setting.

Low for long, slow, all-day, or overnight cooking – great for putting a meal in the pot before you go out for the day or go to bed.

High if you want to speed up the cooking time – generally takes half the time of the low setting.

You can use a combination of low and high if you want to add, say, thickeners to a recipe at the end of the cooking time – simply switch to high for the time specified in your recipe.

Auto Available on some models – this setting automatically switches the cooker from high to low after about 1 hour and enables you to reach the optimum temperature more quickly and reduce the cooking time slightly. If your model does not include this setting you can start the recipe on the high setting for 1 hour and then switch to the low setting manually, adjusting the cooking time accordingly.

Warm At the end of the cooking time this setting can be used to keep the food at the correct serving temperature. Never use this setting for cooking.

USING A SLOW COOKER

Always follow the manufacturer's instructions supplied with your cooker because the actual method of use can vary from model to model.

Some manufacturers recommend preheating the cooker on the high setting 20–30 minutes before adding the food. Others say to heat the pot only when you are about to add the food.

The recipes in this book have not included a preheating instruction. If your instruction manual states that this must be carried out it is important that you do so.

CAPACITIES

Make sure your cooker is at least half full when cooking stews, curries and soups and no more than three-quarters full. Always leave some headroom and never fill the pot right to the top.

PRE-COOKING

When using your cooker to make vegetarian/vegan dishes, pre-cooking ingredients is not essential, yet I do find frying or sautéeing some vegetables, such as onions and aubergines/eggplants, before adding them to the pot is preferable flavourwise, and also ensures they soften properly. If using whole spices, which I also find preferable in a slow cooker, I like to toast them first to enhance their flavour. Pre-cooking can be done in a separate frying pan/skillet or, alternatively, directly in the pot if it can be used on the hob/stovetop.

LIFTING THE LID

Don't be tempted to lift the lid and stir the food. Food won't stick and burn or boil over in a slow cooker. It is said that every time you lift the lid you have to add 20 minutes to the cooking time to compensate for the drop in temperature, although I find with my slow cooker this is slightly exaggerated and if I don't dilly dally leaving the lid off for too long, the effect on timing is negligible. Ideally, only lift the lid if stated in the recipe, and then make sure it is replaced promptly.

COOKING TIMES

All the recipes in this book include a range of cooking times. This means that the food will be cooked and ready to eat at the lower time, but it can be left without spoiling for the maximum time given. Always cook for the minimum time given in the recipe but adjust times according to your own particular model. Some cook faster and some cook slower – especially if you have an older slow cooker.

The cooking times can also be affected by conditions in your kitchen. If the kitchen is very hot you may find that the cooking times are shorter. If it's a very cold day the food may need longer cooking. Similarly, if the slow cooking pot has been refrigerated, let it come to room temperature before cooking. Slow cooking is not an exact science and since certain variables can affect the cooking performance it's a good idea to factor these in when following timings.

Cooking times will vary but approximate comparative cooking times on low and high are as follows:

Low setting	High setting
4–8 hours	1½–4 hours
7–9 hours	5–6 hours
9–10 hours	7–8 hours

Slow cooker size guide:

SIZE	MAX CAPACITY	SERVINGS
Small	1.5 litres /2½ pints/1.5 quarts	1–2 servings Ideal for couples or 1 to 2 person households
Medium	3.5 litres/6 pints/4 quarts	3–4 servings (depending on the recipe) Ideal for small families
Large	6.5 litres/11½ pints/6 quarts	6–8 servings Great for larger quantities and batch cooking

HEALTHY SLOW COOKER

VEGETABLES

Vegetables are the ultimate health food and ideally should play a major part of each meal. To benefit from the widest range of nutrients, phytochemicals and antioxidants, try to eat a good variety of fresh produce in a range of colours.

Most types of vegetable can be successfully cooked in a slow cooker – starchy root vegetables, such as carrots, turnips/rutabagas, parsnips, potatoes, swede and celeriac benefit from slow cooking and work well in curries, stews and one-pot meals. Aubergines/eggplants, tomatoes, (bell) peppers and courgettes/zucchini become meltingly soft if cooked for long periods in a sauce, stock or olive oil. Conversely, leafy veg including spinach, kale, cavolo nero and chard, should be added towards the end of the cooking time to preserve their nutrient value and texture. For convenience, make use of frozen veg, especially if the fresh equivalent is out of season, but do defrost it first and cook until heated through.

There is patchy, if any, respected research on nutrient loss from food that is cooked for long periods, but nutritionally some vegetables respond better to being cooked than eaten raw. For instance, cooking enhances the antioxidant content of tomatoes; while combining them with a fat, such as olive oil, increases the body's ability to absorb certain nutrients found in the fruit.

Slow cooking is a gentle way to cook and since temperatures are kept below boiling point (see page 10), it is arguable that more nutrients are preserved than when vegetables are cooked rapidly at a high heat, such as when boiled, grilled/broiled or fried.

The beauty of cooking in a slow cooker is that a lot of vegetables don't need to be peeled and since many nutrients are found in, or just below, the skin this is no bad thing (the skin also provides valuable fibre).

Make use of sea vegetables in your slow cooking, too. For instance, nori, wakame and kombu are incredibly rich in minerals such as iodine, zinc, calcium, magnesium, manganese, potassium and trace elements including selenium. Dried nori or wakame can be sprinkled over dishes, while kombu added to a cooking pot of dried beans will help soften them and curb any unwanted side effects.

Preparation/cooking tips

• Some vegetables – especially root vegetables such as carrots, beetroot/beets, turnips/rutabagas and parsnips can take longer to cook than meat in most cookers so cut into small even-sized dice, slices or bite-sized pieces according to the recipe.

• Add delicate vegetables such as broccoli, asparagus and leafy greens towards the end of the cooking time to avoid overcooking and loss of colour and nutrients. Baby spinach and chopped kale can just be added at the end and stirred through the mixture – they will cook in the heat of the food.

• Cut potatoes tend to discolour if not submerged in the cooking liquid so push them down into the pot.

PULSES/DRIED BEANS

Beans and pulses respond beautifully to slow cooking. These humble ingredients are relatively inexpensive to buy and brimming with nutrients, vitamins, minerals and fibre, including folic acid, magnesium, iron, potassium and B vitamins. They are also rich in both complex carbohydrates and protein so should be one of your go-to ingredients for good health. (Both the American Heart Association and American Cancer Society recommend beans and pulses as one of the most important food groups for disease prevention.)

In the main, the recipes specify 'cooked' beans, and these can either be from a can or cooked from their dried soaked form, although the latter are more economical to use. Usually the ratio of cooked versus dried is 2:1, for instance, if a recipe specifies 100 g/3½ oz. canned beans, you will need to start with 50 g/1¾ oz. dried beans. Remember, too, that a 400-g/14-oz. can beans contains around 200 g/7 oz. beans, when drained.

Dried beans and pulses should be soaked (see right), since not only does this speed up the cooking time, it helps to improve their digestibility. Lentils don't require pre-soaking or cooking and can simply be added to the pot after a good rinse to remove any impurities.

If put off by the gaseous after-effect of beans, add a strip of dried kombu seaweed to the cooking pot – ginger, fennel or cumin can help, too, as well as boosting the nutrient content of the dish. Alongside their health benefits, pulses add extra substance to your cooking and can also act as a type of thickener.

Preparation/cooking tip

• Pulses and dried beans contain a toxin that must be removed before cooking. The following method MUST be carried out before they can be cooked in the slow cooker. It is advisable to carry out this method of preparation for all varieties when cooking in the slow cooker even if the pack instructions say that this is not necessary. Pulses and dried beans MUST be soaked overnight in plenty of cold water to soften them. After soaking, drain them and put into a pan with fresh water. Bring to the boil, then boil rapidly for 10 minutes. I recommend boiling for an additional 10 minutes to tenderise them at this stage, then drain and add to the slow cooker.

• The only exceptions to this rule are red, green, brown and Puy lentils. These do not need to be soaked and boiled before adding to the slow cooker.

• Do not add salt to pulses and dried beans until the end of the cooking time as it toughens them.

FRUIT

Most of the recipes in this book are savoury, with the exception of a few breakfast dishes. That said, fresh and dried fruits are added to some of the savoury stews and curries to enhance their flavour, texture and nutritional value. When possible, avoid peeling fresh fruit to retain its fibre content as well as nutrients found in, or just below, the skin.

Although dried fruit is super-sweet, it is a good source of iron, magnesium, potassium and calcium. Similarly, the fibre content is higher than in fresh.

Preparation/cooking tip

• Dried and fresh fruit cook well, retaining colour, texture and flavour.

RICE & GRAINS

Some cookery experts recommend easy cook/quick cook rice in a slow cooker since the grains retain their shape and texture. I've also found that brown jasmine rice works very well. It has a shorter grain than basmati, but nevertheless cooks evenly and retains its shape. It also has a lovely nutty flavour.

Opt for brown wholegrain rice instead of refined white – it's a better source of fibre, vitamins and minerals, including magnesium, selenium and manganese, and is surprisingly high in antioxidants. Additionally, it is a low glycaemic food, which means that it helps to keep blood-sugar levels stable.

Other wholegrains such as barley, faro, spelt and jumbo oats also hold their own when slow cooked without turning mushy. They provide a catalogue of beneficial nutrients as well as fibre, which aids digestive health, improving nutrient absorption, immunity and promoting good bacteria in the gut.

Preparation/cooking tips

• Rinse rice and grains well before use.

• Use coarser jumbo oats for porridge to give a good consistency, rather than quick cook or fine cut oats, which can become a bit mushy.

• Always eat rice as soon as it is cooked and do not leave it sitting at room temperature – cooked rice contains spores that can cause food poisoning if not handled correctly. If you are not eating rice or a rice dish immediately, remove from the pot at the end of the cooking time, cool as quickly as possible (ideally within 1 hour) and store in the fridge.

• Don't leave cooked rice on the slow cooker 'keep warm' setting for food safety reasons and also to avoid overcooking it.

FATS

Slow cooking can be a low-fat method of food preparation. When cooking soups and stews, for instance, it's perfectly feasible to bung the main ingredients into the pot without adding any oil or fat. That said, the right fats provide numerous health benefits and are essential for the body to function normally – some vitamins need the presence of fat to be absorbed by the body.

Recently, there's been a review in thinking by health experts relating to fats and health, with studies showing that saturated fat may be better for us than previously thought. It appears that there is now insufficient evidence to support the theory that saturated fat increases the risk of heart disease.

Coconut oil and ghee (clarified butter) are used in the recipes for curries and Asian-style dishes. Both are stable oils when heated and offer a range of health benefits, too. Coconut oil has a strong, distinctive flavour that suits Asian dishes and is rich in medium-chain fatty acids. It is said to be antiviral, antifungal and antibacterial as well as helping to increase levels of good cholesterol in the body. This promotes good heart health and helps improve brain and memory function. Look for extra-virgin unrefined coconut oil, which is purer and the best quality.

Ghee is a very stable fat and is rich in fat-soluble vitamins and minerals, including the antioxidant selenium. Find it in jars in the world food section in supermarkets or in Asian grocers.

Olive oil is also used in the book and as a monounsaturated fat it is rich in antioxidants and is good for the health of the heart and cognitive function. I tend to go for extra-virgin, rather than just virgin, as it has a better flavour and is a good multi-functional oil.

Other types of beneficial fats in the book include butter, dairy and cold-pressed rapeseed oil, which is a world away from regular highly processed rapeseed oil. There is a whole host of non-dairy butters and spreads now available and they are worth checking out. They are largely interchangeable with dairy butters, but do check the packet first.

Preparation/cooking tips

• Remove any excess oil from the surface at the end of cooking using kitchen paper/paper towels or a skimmer, if preferred.

• Try to buy the best quality oil you can afford for the best results in your cooking – they are likely to have a better flavour and be best for your health as they are less refined and blended.

HERBS, SPICES & SALT

Herbs and spices not only lift and enhance the flavour and interest of a dish, they benefit our health, too. Herbs such as basil, coriander/cilantro, bay, dill, mint, oregano and thyme, are all said to aid digestion and have a carminative effect on the stomach, easing indigestion and nausea. Similarly, many spices are renowned for their digestive properties.

Additionally, spices help to reduce the need for salt in cooking as they significantly enhance the flavour of food. They also feature a wide range of antioxidants and are believed to increase metabolism, particularly chilli/chile, which has been found to aid weight loss.

Ginger is excellent for digestion and gastro problems, particularly nausea. An anti-inflammatory, it has been found to reduce the symptoms of, and pain associated with, arthritis.

Turmeric could be hailed as the spice of the moment, but it has been revered in Asian and Middle Eastern countries for many hundreds of years, particularly as an anti-inflammatory and digestive. Numerous studies also suggest it has antioxidant, antiviral and antibacterial properties. Curcumin is the active ingredient and is more

bioavailable if consumed with piperine, a compound found in black pepper. Buy turmeric in root or in dried powdered form – organic is best if you can find it.

Sea salt is used throughout the book, rather than highly processed table salt. Rich in trace minerals, it promotes balanced acid/alkaline levels in the body and restores electrolyte balance. Do be mindful of the amount you consume.

Preparation/cooking tips

• Fresh herbs can easily become overcooked, losing their flavour, so add them at the end.

• Dried herbs are more robust so can be added at the beginning of the cooking process.

• Spices can also lose some of their flavour during slow cooking so add more according to your taste to compensate for this.

• Whole spices tend to have a better flavour than ready ground, which can become stale over time. Whole spices also benefit from toasting first to enhance their flavour. This can be done before adding to the slow cooker, simply toast them in a dry frying pan/skillet over a medium-low heat for 1–2 minutes, tossing the pan occasionally, until they smell aromatic. They can either be used whole or ground in a grinder, mini food processor or using a pestle and mortar depending on the recipe

LIQUIDS

Many of the recipes in this book feature vegetable stock/broth. You can use ready-made but here is a recipe for a basic vegetable stock/broth that is cheap to prepare, makes use of leftovers and waste, and comes without unwanted additives.

Cooking/preparation tips

• This vegetable stock/broth uses mushrooms, but they can be swapped for parsnips, tomatoes, leeks and/or fennel, or to increase the mushroomy flavour add dried porcini. To intensify the flavour of the stock/broth, roast the onions, carrots and celery first. Heat 1 tablespoon olive oil in a pan/skillet and sauté 2 sliced onions for 8 minutes, stirring, until softened. Add 3 sliced carrots, 3 sliced garlic cloves, 2 sliced celery sticks/ribs and 175 g/6¼ oz. sliced chestnut mushrooms and cook for a further 5 minutes. Tip everything in the slow cooker pot and add 1.5 litres/6 cups just-boiled water, 1 large handful of parsley stalks, 3 bay leaves and ½ tsp black peppercorns. Cover and cook for 6–7 hours on low or 4–5 hours on high, until the vegetables are tender. Strain through a sieve/strainer, discarding the bay leaves, and press the solids through the sieve/strainer with the back of a spoon. Season the stock/broth with salt. To concentrate the flavour of the stock/broth, return it to the slow cooker pot and cook it on high, uncovered, until reduced. Leave to cool and store, covered, in the fridge for up to 5 days or 3 months in the freezer.

• To ensure the correct temperatures are reached safely it is important to use hot stock/both or water in most cases. This helps to give a boost in temperature at the start of the cooking process and reduces the cooking time, if desired.

• There is very little evaporation from a slow cooker so less liquid may be needed. If you find there is too much liquid at the end of the cooking time, simply remove the lid and cook on high for about 30 minutes until the liquid has reduced.

BREAKFAST & BRUNCH

SLOW-COOKED MIXED GRAIN PORRIDGE

If leaving a pot of porridge to cook overnight fills you with slight trepidation, don't worry the bain marie/water bath stops it drying out – what's more, you'll wake up to the luxury of a pot of creamy, comforting porridge. The rye flakes add a bit of extra bite to the porridge, but you can use just oats, if preferred. I was shocked to read recently that oats are one of the most pesticide-sprayed grains around, so do opt for organic.

butter or dairy-free
   alternative, for
   greasing
75 g/¾ cup jumbo
   porridge oats
25 g/¼ cup rye flakes
   (or just use 100 g/
   1 cup oats)
½ tsp ground
   cinnamon, plus
   extra for serving
1 large pinch of sea
   salt
325 ml/1⅓ cups cold
   milk, dairy or
   alternative, plus
   extra to serve

TO SERVE
1 handful of pecans,
   roughly broken
1 tsp milled chia seeds
2 handfuls of
   blueberries
6 dried figs, roughly
   chopped

Low 7 hours
High 2½–3 hours

Serves 2–3

Liberally grease a heatproof 1 litre/4 cups plus 3 tbsp deep bowl or dish that fits into your slow cooker pot – I like to use an oval-shaped, stoneware casserole dish. Mix together the oats and rye, if using, cinnamon and salt. Pour over your cold milk of choice and 300 ml/1¼ cups cold water, stir, then transfer to the slow cooker pot.

Pour enough cold water around the bowl or dish to come three-quarters of the way up the side. (If cooking on high for the shorter time, add just-boiled water from the kettle.)

Cover and cook for 7 hours on low or 2½–3 hours on high.

When the porridge is cooked, carefully lift out the dish with oven gloves and give it a good stir to remove any crusty bits around the edge. Spoon into bowls and top with the pecans, chia seeds, blueberries and figs and finish with extra milk, if liked, and a sprinkling of cinnamon.

BREAKFAST BROWN RICE PUDDING

Is it a tad indulgent to eat rice pudding for breakfast – well why not? The beauty
of using brown rice, rather than white, in this pudding is that it can be cooked low and
slow overnight, ready to enjoy for breakfast. What's more, as a wholegrain, brown rice
is a good source of beneficial fibre as well as magnesium and folate. The topping
is just a suggestion, do opt for your own favourite fruit, nuts and seeds – or it's just
as good served with extra hot milk.

butter or dairy-free
  alternative, for
  greasing
120 g/1²/₃ cup brown
  pudding rice
1 litre/4 cups
  whole milk or
  unsweetened
  almond or oat milk
1 tsp vanilla bean
  paste
25 g/1¾ tbsp light soft
  brown sugar
¼ tsp freshly grated
  nutmeg, plus extra
  to serve

TO SERVE
Overnight Orchard
  Fruit Jam (see page
  27), or preferred
  seasonal fresh fruit
1 handful of walnuts,
  roughly broken
  (optional)
cream, or dairy-free
  alternative,
  if you're feeling
  really indulgent
  (optional)

Low 7 hours
High 2½–3½ hours

Serves 3–4

Generously grease the base and the sides of the
slow cooker pot and add the rice.

Mix together the milk, vanilla, brown sugar and
nutmeg and pour it over the rice, then stir briefly
until combined. Cover and cook for 7 hours on
low. If you want the rice pudding to cook more
quickly, so not overnight, use warm milk instead
of cold and cook for 2½–3½ hours on high. When
ready, the rice is tender and the milk thickened
slightly, but the pudding is still quite loose.

Top each serving with a spoonful of the overnight
orchard fruit jam or fruit of choice as well as
walnuts. Finish with a swirl of cream, if using,
and an extra grating of nutmeg.

CHINESE RICE PORRIDGE

This savoury rice porridge, or congee, is made with short-grain brown jasmine rice, flavoured with stock/broth and fresh root ginger. I like it topped with a soft-boiled egg, spring onion/scallion, nori and a splash of sesame oil and soy sauce but do choose your own favourite toppings. The rice porridge can be cooked slowly overnight to a thick, soupy consistency, although you could cook it more quickly using hot stock/broth. Soothing, reviving and nutritious, it makes the perfect comfort food – breakfast, lunch or dinner – if you're feeling below par.

150 g/¾ cup short-grain brown jasmine rice, rinsed well
1 thumb-sized piece of fresh root ginger, peeled and thickly sliced
1 litre/4 cups cold vegetable stock/broth (see page 17)
freshly ground black pepper

TO SERVE
4 soft-boiled eggs, halved, and/or fried sliced mushrooms
2 spring onions/scallions, thinly sliced diagonally
2 tsp nori or dulse flakes
2 tsp chilli/chile bean sauce
sesame oil and soy sauce, for drizzling

Low 7–8 hours
High 2½–3½ hours

Serves 4

Put the rice in the slow cooker pot with the ginger and pour over the stock/broth and 500 ml/2 cups cold water – it will look as though there is a lot of liquid, but don't worry. Cover and cook for 7–8 hours on low or 2½–3½ hours on high, using hot stock/broth and just-boiled water from the kettle, until the rice is very tender and the grains start to break down. It should be fairly loose and soupy in consistency. Season with pepper to taste – you shouldn't need any salt.

Remove the ginger and ladle the rice porridge into bowls. Top each serving with an egg and/or fried mushrooms, spring onions/scallions, nori or dulse flakes, chilli/chile bean sauce and a final drizzle of sesame oil and soy sauce. Chopped peanuts and fresh coriander/cilantro are also good additions.

For a sweet version, replace the stock/broth with water or half water/half milk, flavoured with a cinnamon stick. Top with fruit, honey, nuts and grated nutmeg.

OVERNIGHT ORCHARD FRUIT JAM

You can cook this fresh jam more quickly, if you prefer, but when cooked slowly and gently overnight on low you'll be rewarded with a rich fruity, indulgent-tasting jam-cum-compote that's perfect on toast or spooned on top of yogurt or porridge. It's a lovely thing to wake up to!

5 red plums, about 270 g/9½ oz. in weight, halved and stones removed
2 large dessert apples, peeled, cored and diced
200 g/generous 1 cup dried apricots, roughly chopped
1 tsp vanilla bean paste

a squeeze of lemon juice

Low 4–7 hours
High 3–5 hours

Makes 500 g/18 oz.

Place the plums, cut-side down, in the slow cooker pot and top with the apples and apricots. Spoon over the vanilla and add the lemon juice and 1 tablespoon water. Cover and cook for 4–7 hours on low or 3–5 hours on high.

Remove the lid and mash with the back of a fork into a rough or smooth purée – depending on your preference (or you can purée in a blender). Spoon into a bowl and serve.

MIXED FRUIT COMPOTE WITH HIBISCUS

Dried hibiscus flowers add a fruity, slightly sour flavour to this compote and contrasts beautifully with the sweetness of the dried fruit. Hibiscus is also loaded with vitamin C and other antioxidants, supporting immunity and the health of our skin, hair and nails. The fruit can be left to cook on low overnight, in which case use cold water. If you want to speed things up, use just-boiled water from the kettle. Serve the rich compote with thick yogurt – nuts and seeds are a good addition too.

250 g/1½ cups mixed dried fruit, such as figs, cherries, apricots
1 cinnamon stick
¼ tsp ground allspice
½ tbsp dried hibiscus flowers
freshly squeezed juice of 1 large orange

thick natural/plain live yogurt, or dairy-free alternative, to serve

Low 7–8 hours
High 3–4 hours

Serves about 6

Put the dried fruit, cinnamon, allspice and hibiscus in the slow cooker pot. Pour in the orange juice and 200 ml/¾ cup cold water and stir until combined. Cover and cook for 7–8 hours on low or 3–4 hours on high, until the fruit is soft and plump. Add more water (hot if you want to serve the compote warm), if you prefer a more saucy consistency, but it is lovely if it becomes thick and syrupy.

Just before serving, pick out the cinnamon stick (give it a rinse and use again) and the hibiscus flowers. Serve warm or cold with yogurt.

CHAI-POACHED PEARS

Pears poach beautifully in a slow cooker and work particularly well with spices, especially immune-supporting ginger. These take minimum effort and make a delicious breakfast with yogurt, sprinkled with granola, or as a make-ahead healthy pudding. Look for pears that are on the firm side, so they keep their shape during cooking.

750 ml/3¼ cups fresh apple juice (not from concentrate)
3 chai herbal tea bags
¼ tsp ground turmeric (optional)
2.5-cm/1-in. piece of fresh root ginger, sliced
1 cinnamon stick
4 pears, peeled and halved

TO SERVE
natural/plain Greek yogurt, or dairy-free alternative
granola

Low 2½–3½ hours
High 1½–2½ hours

Serves 4

Gently heat the apple juice in a small pan with the herbal tea bags, turmeric, if using, ginger and cinnamon. When warm, turn off the heat and leave to infuse for 30 minutes. Remove the tea bags but leave the ginger and cinnamon in the juice.

Arrange the pears in the slow cooker pot – they should fit in a single layer. Pour the apple juice mixture over the pears until they are submerged in the liquid. Cover and cook for 2½–3½ hours on low or 1½–2½ hours on high, until tender. Remove the pears with a slotted spoon. To reduce the spiced juice, pour it into a small pan (or keep it in the slow cooker pan if it can go on a hob/stovetop) and cook until reduced and syrupy.

Serve the pears with some of the juices spooned over, Greek yogurt and a sprinkling of granola.

SHAKSHUKA-OF-SORTS

A popular easy breakfast dish in the Middle East and North Africa, the beauty of this dish is that the lightly spiced tomato sauce can gently simmer on low overnight, then quickly finished off in the morning with the addition of eggs. I prefer to cook the eggs separately – either poached or fried – hence the 'of sorts' in the recipe title. This way it's much easier to cook them to everyone's liking, but if you prefer to the traditional method cooking them in the sauce, I've given instructions for both.

1½ tsp cumin seeds

1 red onion, finely chopped

2 garlic cloves, finely chopped

250 g/8¾ oz. roasted red (bell) peppers from a jar, drained and rinsed if in vinegar, roughly chopped

1½ x 400-g/14-oz. cans chopped tomatoes

1 bay leaf

1 tbsp extra-virgin olive oil

4 eggs

sea salt and freshly ground black pepper

TO SERVE

dried chilli/hot pepper flakes

Tahini Yogurt (see page 116) (optional)

Low 7–8 hours
High 4–5 hours

Serves 4

Toast the cumin seeds in a dry frying pan/skillet over a medium-low heat for 1 minute, tossing the pan/skillet occasionally. Tip the seeds into the slow cooker pot.

Add the onion, garlic, roasted red (bell) peppers, chopped tomatoes, bay leaf and olive oil. Season with salt and pepper to taste. Cover and cook for 7–8 hours on low or for 4–5 hours on high.

To poach the eggs, half-fill a sauté pan with cold water and heat until gently simmering. Swirl the water and reduce the heat to low. Crack the eggs, one at a time, into the pan and cook for 3–4 minutes, until the white is set but the yolk remains runny. (Alternatively, make 4 small wells in the sauce and crack an egg into each one – if the sauce is too loose to hold an indent, don't worry the eggs can be cracked on top. Cover with the lid and cook for 15 minutes on high.)

Serve the tomato sauce topped with an egg, a sprinkling of chilli/hot pepper flakes and a spoonful of tahini yogurt, if you like. Crusty bread is good for mopping up the juices.

BREAKFAST BEAN BURRITOS

A pot of pinto beans will happily simmer away overnight, ready to be enjoyed the next day for breakfast or brunch as part of a Mexican-style spread. Let everyone build their own burrito – you could also add quinoa to the mix for a more substantial meal; the multi-coloured one is a favourite of mine.

BURRITO FILLING

200 g/generous 1 cup
    pinto beans, rinsed
    and soaked for
    8 hours
1 large red onion,
    grated
1 tbsp extra-virgin
    olive oil, plus extra
    for drizzling
2 garlic cloves, grated
2 tbsp tomato purée/
    paste
2 tsp ground cumin
2 tsp hot smoked
    paprika
½ tsp dried chipotle
    flakes or paste
½ tsp dried thyme
500 ml/2 cups just-
    boiled water from
    the kettle
1 tsp vegetable
    bouillon powder
sea salt and freshly
    ground black
    pepper

TO SERVE

5 vine-ripened
    tomatoes, deseeded
    and diced
1 handful of chopped
    coriander/cilantro
    leaves
2 limes, quartered
2 small avocados,
    stone and skin
    removed, sliced
    lengthways
150 g/1¼ cup feta,
    crumbled (optional)
8 small corn tortillas,
    warmed in a low
    oven, or in a ridged
    skillet set over low
    heat

Low 8–9 hours
High 5–6 hours

Serves 4

Put the soaked pinto beans in a pan and cover with cold water. Bring to the boil over a high heat, then leave to bubble away for 10 minutes, skimming off any white froth on the surface. Turn the heat down slightly and simmer for another 10 minutes. Drain the beans and tip them into the slow cooker pot.

Grate three-quarters of the onion and save the remainder to serve. Add to the slow cooker pot with the oil, garlic, tomato purée/paste, cumin, smoked paprika, chipotle, thyme and hot water. Stir in the bouillon powder. Cover with the lid and cook for 8–9 hours on low (if you want to cook them overnight opt for the longer time) or 5–6 hours on high, until the beans are tender. Season with salt and pepper, to taste, then mash half the beans to break them down using a potato masher or the back of a fork.

To serve, finely dice the remaining red onion and put it in a bowl with the tomatoes and coriander/cilantro. Season with salt and add a good squeeze of lime juice. Place the avocado on a separate serving plate and squeeze over some lime juice to stop it turning brown. Crumble the feta into a bowl.

Let everyone help themselves, spooning a good helping of the beans onto a warm tortilla and topping it with a few slices of avocado, the tomato, salsa and a sprinkling of feta, if using. Finish with a drizzle of olive oil and a squeeze of lime juice.

MEAT-FREE SLOPPY JOES

Crumbled tempeh, rather than the more usual minced beef, is used to make the filling for this popular American sandwich. Tempeh is perfect as it retains its soya bean texture and readily takes on the smoky tomato flavours of the other filling ingredients. It's also a good source of bone-friendly minerals, such as calcium and magnesium, as well as beneficial fibre. This makes a perfect brunch but be warned, they're deliciously messy to eat as their name suggests.

20 g/1½ tbsp butter or dairy-free alternative, or extra-virgin olive oil
1 onion, finely chopped
1 small green (bell) pepper, deseeded and chopped
2 garlic cloves, finely chopped
200 g/7 oz. tempeh, crumbled
3 tbsp tomato purée/paste
1½ tsp chipotle paste
2 tbsp tomato ketchup
1½ tbsp soy sauce
1 tsp English mustard
sea salt and freshly ground black pepper

TO SERVE
4 brioche buns or soft wholegrain seedy buns, split in half
4 Little Gem lettuce leaves
40 g/½ cup Cheddar or other hard cheese or dairy-free alternative, grated (optional)
1 tbsp drained jalapeño chillies/chiles from a jar

Low 7 hours
High 2–3 hours

Serves 4

Heat the butter or olive oil in a frying pan/skillet over a medium heat and fry the onion and (bell) pepper for 7 minutes, until softened. Add the garlic and cook for another 2 minutes, stirring. Stir in the tempeh.

Meanwhile, mix together the tomato purée/paste, chipotle paste, ketchup, soy sauce, mustard and 200 ml/¾ cup cold water in a jug/pitcher until combined.

Add the tempeh mixture to the slow cooker pot, pour in the sauce and stir until combined. Cover with the lid and cook for 7 hours on low if cooking overnight (you can cook this in less time on low, about 3–4 hours, if using just-boiled water from the kettle instead of cold), or 2–3 hours on high using hot water.

To assemble, lightly toast the buns under the grill/broiler or in a ridged skillet. Place a lettuce leaf, facing upwards, on the bottom half of each bun and top with a generous spoonful of the tempeh mixture. Scatter the cheese over, if using, and finish with the jalapeños and bun tops. Serve straightaway with plenty of paper napkins.

SOUPS & BROTHS

SQUASH & GINGER SOUP

The Japanese kuri with its slightly sweet, creamy flavour is my squash of choice, but feel free to swap it for your favourite variety of squash or pumpkin. In terms of flavour, squash is also the perfect counter to the heat of the fresh ginger. The spice's ability to calm nausea and digestive problems are well known, but these are just two in a long list of positives for this wonder root. Loaded with antioxidants, ginger is also said to be good for the health of the lungs.

1 tbsp coconut oil, plus a little extra melted to serve
1 large onion, coarsely grated
1 celery stick/rib, diced
2 carrots, diced
750 g/1 lb. 10 oz. kuri squash, or any favourite squash or pumpkin, peeled, deseeded and cut into 2-cm/1-in. chunks
90 g/½ cup split red lentils, rinsed well
½ tsp ground turmeric
1.2 litres/5 cups hot vegetable stock/broth
2 bay leaves
1 thumb-sized piece of fresh root ginger, cut into 1-cm/½-in. rounds
1 tsp cumin seeds, toasted (optional)
1 medium-hot red chilli/chile, thinly sliced
sea salt and freshly ground black pepper

Low 3½–4½ hours
High 2½–3½ hours

Serves 4

Put the coconut oil, onion, celery, carrots, squash and lentils in the slow cooker pot. Mix the turmeric into the hot stock/broth and pour into the pot. Tuck in the bay leaves and ginger. Cover and cook for 3½–4½ hours on low or 2½–3½ hours on high, until the lentils and vegetables are tender.

Pick out the bay leaves and ginger. Blend the soup in a blender or using a hand stick blender and season with salt and pepper to taste. Ladle into four bowls and top with a drizzle of melted coconut oil, a sprinkling of toasted cumin seeds, if using, and chilli/chile slices.

MOROCCAN LENTIL SOUP

They may be small, but lentils are nutritionally impressive, providing plentiful amounts of gut-supporting fibre as well as B vitamins and minerals, such as zinc, iron and potassium. Lentils also cook beautifully in a slow cooker – it's a method of cooking that suits them and these brown lentils retain their shape while soaking up the flavour of the spices.

1 large onion, finely chopped

1 celery stick/rib, finely chopped

4 carrots, cut into 4 lengthways, then sliced into 2-cm/ 1-in. chunks

150 g/¾ cup brown lentils, rinsed

1 tsp ground turmeric

2 tsp ras el hanout

1 tsp hot smoked paprika

1.2 litres/5 cups hot vegetable stock/ broth

2 tbsp tomato purée/ paste

2 bay leaves

2 tbsp extra-virgin olive oil, plus extra for drizzling

100 g/3⅓ cups spinach leaves, roughly chopped

juice of ½ lemon, freshly squeezed

sea salt and freshly ground black pepper

TO SERVE

Tahini Yogurt (see page 116) (optional)

1 medium-hot green chilli/chile, sliced into thin rounds

Low 5–6 hours
High 3–4 hours

Serves 4

Put the onion, celery, carrots, lentils, spices, hot stock/broth, tomato purée/paste and bay leaves in the slow cooker pot. Cover and cook for 5–6 hours on low or for 3–4 hours on high.

Fifteen minutes before the end of the cooking time, quickly stir in the olive oil, spinach and lemon juice, taking care not to lose too much heat in the pot. Cover and cook until wilted.

Season with salt and pepper to taste and serve topped with a spoonful of the tahini yogurt, if you like, the sliced green chilli/chile and an extra drizzle of olive oil.

JERUSALEM ARTICHOKE & ROSEMARY SOUP

Jerusalem artichokes can be a little bit of a fiddle to peel, but it's really worth trying them for the comforting sweet, nutty flavour they give to soups, stews and purées – they're delicious roasted too. This winter root vegetable also comes with an impressive list of health benefits. Rich in soluble fibre and inulin, the latter is a prebiotic that supports digestive health and they're also rich in certain minerals, including magnesium, calcium, iron and potassium. Be warned they can be a bit windy!

20 g/1½ tbsp butter or dairy-free alternative, cut into small pieces

1 large onion, finely chopped

1 large garlic clove, finely chopped

400 g/2½ cups Jerusalem artichokes, peeled and cut into small pieces

1 x 400-g/14-oz. can butter/lima beans, drained

½ tbsp finely chopped rosemary, plus extra to serve

2 bay leaves

600 ml/2½ cups hot vegetable stock/broth

400 ml/1¾ cups milk of choice, dairy or alternative, warmed

2 tbsp cream, dairy or alternative and/or olive oil

sea salt and freshly ground black pepper

Low 3½–4½ hours
High 2½–3½ hours

Serves 4

Put the butter in the bottom of the slow cooker pot and top with the onion, garlic, Jerusalem artichokes, butter/lima beans, rosemary, bay leaves and hot stock/broth, making sure the latter covers the vegetables. If not, poke, them down into the liquid. Cover and cook for 3½–4½ hours on low or 2½–3½ hours on high, until the artichokes are tender.

Thirty minutes before the end of the cooking time, pour in the milk and heat through. Remove the bay leaves and blend the soup until smooth and creamy. Add salt and pepper to taste. Ladle into bowls and top with a swirl of cream and/or olive oil, extra chopped rosemary and a grinding of black pepper.

TUSCAN BREAD & BEAN SOUP

This has everything you could want from a nutritious, sustaining and substantial soup – plentiful amounts of veg, beans, herbs, spices and good-quality bread – and if you are adding vegetarian Parmesan and have a spare rind it's worth adding it to the pot to add another level of flavour.

2 tbsp extra-virgin olive oil, plus extra for drizzling
1 large onion, diced
2 carrots, diced
2 celery sticks/ribs, diced
2 large garlic cloves, finely chopped
¾ tsp fennel seeds
½ tsp dried chilli/hot pepper flakes
2 bay leaves
400-g/14-oz. can cannellini beans, drained
1½ x 400-g/14-oz. can cherry tomatoes
700 ml/3 cups hot vegetable stock/ broth
150 g/5 oz. cavolo nero, tough stalks removed, leaves torn into pieces

3 thick slices day-old Italian country-style bread, about 135 g/4¾ oz. total weight, crusts removed, torn into chunks
freshly squeezed juice of ½ lemon
1 handful of roughly chopped flat-leaf parsley
1 handful of freshly grated vegetarian Parmesan or dairy-free alternative
sea salt and freshly ground black pepper

Low 3½–4½ hours
High 2½–3½ hours

Serves 4

Heat the oil in a large frying pan/skillet over a medium heat. Add the onion, carrots and celery and sauté for 7 minutes, until softened. Add the garlic and fennel seeds and cook for another 2 minutes, stirring.

Transfer the vegetable mix to the slow cooker pot with the chilli/hot pepper flakes, bay leaves, cannellini beans, cherry tomatoes and hot stock/ broth. Cover and cook for 3½ –4½ hours on low or 2½–3½ hours on high.

Fifteen minutes before the end of the cooking time, quickly stir in the cavolo nero so you don't lose too much heat from the pot, pressing the leaves into the stock/broth. Cover and continue to cook until the cavolo nero is tender.

Turn off the heat, stir in the bread and lemon juice. Season with salt and pepper, to taste, and leave to sit for 5 minutes to allow the soup to soak into the bread. Ladle into large shallow bowls and top with the parsley and Parmesan and a good drizzle of olive oil.

PERSIAN MUNG BEAN SOUP

This is based on a traditional Persian recipe and is a hearty, healthy combination of mung beans, turnip/rutabaga – or use kohlrabi – leeks, noodles and spinach with a good smattering of fresh herbs. You could also top it with a spoonful of soured cream and crispy onions for a bit of crunch. Mung beans are one of the few beans that don't require pre-soaking and cooking, while also being a rich source of minerals, antioxidants and fibre.

2 tbsp extra-virgin olive oil, plus extra for drizzling
1 onion, finely chopped
2 garlic cloves, thinly sliced
2 leeks, thinly sliced
75 g/heaped ⅓ cup mung beans, rinsed well
2 turnips/rutabagas, peeled and cut into 1.5-cm/½-in. chunks
1.2 litres/5 cups hot vegetable stock/broth
½ tsp ground turmeric
70 g/2½ oz. dried vermicelli noodles
110 g/heaped 1¾ cups baby spinach leaves

1 handful of dill sprigs, plus extra to serve
freshly squeezed juice of ½–1 lime
1 tbsp chopped mint leaves
sea salt and freshly ground black pepper

Low 5–6 hours
High 4–5 hours

Serves 4

Heat the olive oil in a frying pan/skillet over a medium heat. Add the onion and fry for 5 minutes, until softened. Add the garlic and cook for another 2 minutes, stirring.

Transfer the onion and garlic to the slow cooker pot with the leeks, mung beans, turnips/rutabagas, hot stock/broth and turmeric, then stir until combined. Cover and cook for 5–6 hours on low or 4–5 hours on high, until the beans and vegetables are tender.

Meanwhile, cook the vermicelli separately in a pan of boiling salted water following the packet instructions, until just al dente, then drain and refresh under cold running water.

Fifteen minutes before the end of the cooking time, quickly stir in the spinach, dill and half of the lime juice. Cover and continue to cook until the spinach wilts. Season with salt and pepper to taste and stir in the cooked vermicelli. Add an extra splash of hot stock/broth, if needed, then turn off the heat and leave to sit for 5 minutes.

Ladle the soup into bowls and top with a drizzle of olive oil, the remaining dill and the mint.

SMOKY SWEETCORN/CORN CHOWDER

This creamy chowder includes beans instead of the more usual potato, which enhance the protein, fibre and carb content. Frozen corn is perfect if fresh is out of season, but make sure you defrost it first.

1 large onion, cut
    into wedges
1 celery stick/rib,
    finely chopped
1 carrot, diced
1 large leek, sliced
3 large garlic cloves,
    finely chopped
1 x 400-g/14-oz. can
    cannellini beans,
    drained and rinsed
2 bay leaves
600 g/3¾ cups corn
    kernels, fresh
    or frozen,
    defrosted if frozen
800 ml/3¼ cups hot
    vegetable stock/
    broth
250 ml/1 cup plus
    1 tbsp hot full-fat/
    whole milk or dairy-
    free alternative
sea salt and freshly
    ground black
    pepper

CHIPOTLE CORN
BUTTER
50 g/3½ tbsp butter
    or dairy-free
    alternative
½–1 tsp chipotle
    paste or flakes

Low 4–5 hours
High 2–3 hours

Serves 4

Char the onion wedges in a large, dry frying pan/skillet over a medium heat for 6 minutes, turning them occasionally, until blackened in places. Leave to cool, then roughly chop.

Add the charred onion to the slow cooker pot with the celery, carrot, leek, garlic, cannellini beans, bay leaves, 500 g/3½ cups of the corn and the hot stock/broth. Cover and cook for 4–5 hours on low or 2–3 hours on high. Pick out the bay leaves, pour in the hot milk and blend the soup until smooth, either in a blender or using a hand stick blender. Season generously with salt and pepper.

To make the chipotle corn butter, pat dry the reserved 100 g/¼ cup corn using kitchen paper/paper towels. Heat a large, dry frying pan/skillet over a medium heat, add the corn and cook, stirring, until blackened in places. Tip into a bowl. Melt the butter in the frying pan/skillet and stir in the chipotle and corn and cook for 1 minute, stirring. Pour the soup into four serving bowls and top with a spoonful of the chipotle corn butter and some freshly ground black pepper.

SHIITAKE RAMEN

Dried shiitake mushrooms make an invaluable addition to the plant-based store cupboard – not only do they add a rich, umami flavour to stocks, stews and broths, like this one, they support immunity and are reputed to have cancer-fighting properties. Additionally, this one-pot meal comes with digestion-supporting miso, ginger, garlic and chilli/chile, while calcium-rich tahini maintains good bone health.

20 g/²⁄₃ cup dried shiitake mushrooms, torn into pieces

2 large banana shallots, chopped

3 garlic cloves, chopped

1 thumb-sized piece of fresh root ginger, peeled and roughly chopped

1 tbsp sesame oil, plus extra for drizzling

1 tbsp soy sauce

3 spring onions/scallions, white and green parts separated, sliced diagonally

2–3 tbsp white miso

2 tbsp tahini

80 g/¾ cup sugar snap peas, halved diagonally

100 g/3½ oz. kale, tough stalks removed, torn into small pieces

500 g/4 cups cooked soba noodles

1 carrot, cut into julienne strips, to serve

1 medium-hot red chilli/chile, thinly sliced diagonally, to serve

2 tsp toasted sesame seeds, to serve

1 tbsp dulse or nori flakes, to serve

Low 2–2½ hours
High 1–1½ hours

Serves 4

Put the dried shiitake in a heatproof bowl and pour over 300 ml/1¼ cups plus 1 tsp just-boiled water from a kettle and leave to hydrate for 30 minutes. Strain the softened shiitake, reserving the soaking liquid. Put the shiitake, shallots, garlic, ginger and 1 tablespoon water in a blender or food processor and blitz to a paste.

Heat the sesame oil in a small frying pan/skillet over a low heat and fry the shiitake paste for 3 minutes, stirring often. Tip the mixture, including any oil, into the slow cooker pot with 900 ml/4 cups just-boiled water from the kettle, the soy sauce and white part of the spring onions/scallions and stir until combined. Cover and cook for 2–2½ hours on low or 1½–2 hours on high.

Fifteen minutes before the end of the cooking time, mix together the miso and tahini and stir into the pot with the sugar snap peas and kale. Cover and finish cooking until the kale has wilted.

Divide the cooked noodles between four large serving bowls. Ladle over the vegetables and broth and top with the carrot, chilli/chile, sesame seeds, green part of the spring onions/scallions, dulse or nori and an extra drizzle of sesame oil.

MUSHROOM DUMPLINGS IN BROTH

This dish is inspired by canederli, the northern Italian bread dumplings, with the traditional cured meat replaced with dried porcini and very untraditional nutritional yeast flakes. The latter are a useful addition to plant-based cooking, adding a 'cheesy' flavour and beneficial amounts of vitamins and minerals. The dumplings are served poached in a light vegetable stock. This recipe requires the high setting to be used.

200 g /7 oz. day-old country-style bread, crusts removed

200 ml/¾ cups milk, dairy or alternative

15 g/½ cup dried porcini mushrooms

40 g/3 tbsp butter or dairy-free alternative

1 onion, very finely chopped

½ tsp dried thyme

4 tbsp nutritional yeast flakes

2 eggs, lightly beaten

plain/all-purpose flour, for dusting

800 ml/3¼ cups hot vegetable stock/ broth

½ recipe quantity Confit Tomatoes (see page 128) (optional)

1 handful of roughly chopped flat-leaf parsley leaves

sea salt and freshly ground black pepper

shaved vegetarian Parmesan or dairy-free alternative, to serve

High 1½–2 hours

Serves 4

Tear the bread into a mixture of small chunks, no bigger than 1 cm/½ in., as well as crumbs. Place the bread chunks and crumbs in a shallow bowl and pour over the milk and leave to soak for 15 minutes.Meanwhile, blitz the dried porcini in a mini food processor or grinder to a powder, then set aside.

Heat 30 g/2 tablespoons of the butter in a frying pan/skillet over a medium-low heat and sauté the onion for 8 minutes, until softened. Leave to cool. Put the thyme, nutritional yeast flakes and ground porcini into a mixing bowl. Squeeze the bread to remove any excess milk, then add to the bowl with the sautéed onion. Add the eggs, season with salt and pepper and mix gently until combined. Pour enough flour onto a plate until it is generously covered.

Pour the hot stock/broth into the slow cooker pot and turn it on to high. With wet hands, form the bread mixture into 12 walnut-sized dumplings. Dunk the dumplings into the flour to lightly coat and pat off any excess. Place the dumplings in the hot stock/broth, spaced evenly apart, there should be some space between them. Cover and cook on high for 1½–2 hours, turning the heat to low if the stock/broth starts to bubble. Scoop the dumplings out and divide between four large, shallow bowls. Add the confit tomatoes, if using, and remaining butter to the stock/broth and stir until the butter melts. Ladle the hot stock/broth over the dumplings and top with the parsley. Season with pepper and finish with shavings of Parmesan.

VIETNAMESE-STYLE BROTH

This pared-back Vietnamese pho makes the perfect work-from-home lunch. Reviving, warming and healthy, just bung the ingredients for the broth into the slow cooker after breakfast and you'll be rewarded with a hot, steaming bowl of soup by lunchtime and a kitchen full with the fragrant aroma of warming spices.

FOR THE BROTH
600 ml/2½ cups just-boiled water from the kettle
1 tsp vegetable bouillon powder
1 star anise
1 thumb-sized piece of fresh root ginger, sliced into thin rounds
1 large garlic clove, thinly sliced
1 medium-hot red chilli/chile, thinly sliced into rounds
2 tsp soy sauce

TO SERVE
Choose from:
150 g/1 scant cup cooked brown rice noodles
2 spring onions/scallions, thinly sliced diagonally
1 tsp dulse or nori flakes
1 carrot, cut into thin strips
1 handful of beansprouts
1 hard-boiled egg, halved
1 small handful of coriander/cilantro leaves
1 small handful of mint leaves

Low 4 hours
High 2 hours

Serves 2

Put all the ingredients for the broth in the slow cooker pot, stir, then cover and cook for 4 hours on low or for 2 hours on high.

Divide the cooked noodles between two bowls, strain the hot, spiced broth over the noodles to heat them, then finish with any combination of your favourite toppings.

BARLEY, ROSEMARY & ROOT VEGETABLE BROTH

Hearty, warming and sustaining, this big bowl soup is loaded with veg and fibre-rich barley – look for pearl, rather than pot barley as it takes less time to cook. The barley softens and helps to thicken the broth as it cooks as well as adding valuable B vitamins, iron and folate.

1 tbsp extra-virgin olive oil, plus extra for drizzling

1 large onion, finely chopped

1 celery stick/rib, diced

2 carrots, halved lengthways and cut into 1-cm/½-in. chunks

½ a small swede, peeled and cut into 1-cm/½-in. chunks

1 parsnip, peeled and cut into 1-cm/½-in. chunks

100 g/½ cup pearl barley, rinsed

2 bay leaves

1 tbsp finely chopped rosemary, plus 1 tsp to serve

1.2 litres/5 cups hot vegetable stock/broth

2 heaped tbsp crème fraîche/sour cream or dairy-free alternative

sea salt and freshly ground black pepper

Low 4–5 hours
High 3–4 hours

Serves 4

Put all the ingredients up to and excluding the crème fraîche in the slow cooker. Cover and cook for 4–5 hours on low or 3–4 hours on high until the barley and vegetables are tender.

Stir in the crème fraîche/sour cream 10 minutes before the end of the cooking time and season generously with salt and pepper. Cover and heat through, adding extra hot vegetable stock/broth if needed. Ladle into bowls and finish with a swirl of olive oil and a little extra chopped rosemary, if you like.

CURRIES & DAHLS

SQUASH, COCONUT & PEA CURRY

Peas not only add a burst of colour to this coconut curry, they provide an impressive number of antioxidant vitamins, including C and E, as well as gut-friendly fibre. Make sure you defrost the peas before adding them to the pot so you don't lose valuable heat. Sweet potato, pumpkin, carrot or other root vegetables make worthy alternatives to the squash.

2 tsp panch phoran spice mix
1 tsp coriander seeds
½ tsp brown mustard seeds
1 tbsp coconut oil
1 large onion, finely chopped
3 large garlic cloves
1 thumb-sized piece of fresh root ginger, grated
250 g/8¾ oz. small tomatoes, halved
800 g/1 lb. 12 oz. butternut squash, peeled, deseeded and cut into 2-cm/1-in. chunks
200 ml/¾ cup just-boiled water from the kettle

200 ml/¾ cup canned coconut milk
2 tsp medium curry powder
1 tsp ground turmeric
160 g/1¼ cups frozen peas, defrosted
squeeze of lemon juice
sea salt and freshly ground black pepper
cooked brown basmati rice, to serve

Low 4–5 hours
High 3–4 hours

Serves 4

Toast the panch phoran, coriander seeds and mustard seeds in a dry frying pan/skillet for 1–2 minutes, tossing the pan occasionally, until they smell aromatic. Tip into a grinder or mini food processor and grind to a powder. Set aside until ready to use.

Heat the coconut oil in the frying pan/skillet over a medium heat and fry the onion for 6 minutes, until softened. Add the garlic and ginger and cook for another 2 minutes, stirring.

Transfer the onion mix to the slow cooker pot with the tomatoes, squash, hot water and coconut milk, then stir until combined. Cover and cook for 4–5 hours on low or 3–4 hours on high, until the squash is tender and starting to break down in places into the sauce.

Twenty minutes before the end of the cooking time, stir in the ground spices and the defrosted peas. Cover and continue to cook until heated through. Add a squeeze of lemon juice and season with salt and pepper to taste before serving with rice.

AUBERGINE/EGGPLANT & SMOKED TOFU MASSAMAN CURRY

Full of aromatic spices, this hearty Thai curry has a richness thanks to the coconut milk – I tend to go for full fat as it adds a lovely creaminess and flavour to the sauce but do opt for the lighter option if watching your fat intake. I also prefer to use toasted whole spices, then grind them, in curries as they hold up to slow cooking better than ready-ground alternatives, which can lose a bit of oomph. However, if going for the latter, add them an hour before the end of the cooking time with the smoked tofu.

2 tsp cumin seeds

2 tsp coriander seeds

2 tbsp coconut oil

2 large banana shallots, finely chopped

2 aubergines/ eggplants, sliced and cut into 2-cm/ 1-in. chunks

3 garlic cloves, finely chopped

400-g/14-oz. can coconut milk

100 g/3½ tbsp Thai red curry paste

50 ml/3 tbsp just-boiled water from the kettle

6 cardamom pods, split

2 lemongrass stalks, outer leaves removed, lightly crushed

200 g/7 oz. new potatoes, scrubbed and quartered

225 g/8 oz. smoked tofu, drained, patted dry and cut into 2-cm/1-in. cubes

freshly squeezed juice of 1 lime

sea salt and freshly ground black pepper

TO SERVE

1 handful each of roasted unsalted peanuts, roughly chopped

coriander/cilantro leaves

brown jasmine rice

wedges of lime

Low 4–5 hours
High 3–4 hours

Serves 4

Toast the cumin and coriander seeds in a large, dry frying pan/skillet for 2 minutes over a medium-low heat, until they smell aromatic. Leave to cool, then grind in a grinder or pestle and mortar. Set aside.

Heat the coconut oil in the frying pan/skillet over a medium heat and add the shallots and aubergines/eggplants and fry, turning often, for 6 minutes, until starting to colour. Add the garlic and cook for another 2 minutes, then tip everything into the slow cooker pot.

Pour 4 tablespoons of the coconut milk into the pan, turn down the heat slightly, and add the red curry paste. Cook, stirring, for 2 minutes, then pour in the rest of the coconut milk and warm through.

Transfer the coconut mixture to the slow cooker pot and stir in the hot water, cardamom, lemongrass and new potatoes. Cover and cook for 4–5 hours on low or 3–4 hours on high. One hour before the curry is finished, quickly stir in the tofu, taking care not to break up the pieces, then cover and finish cooking.

When ready to serve, remove the lemongrass and add the lime juice. Season with salt and pepper to taste. Serve topped with the peanuts and coriander/cilantro, with rice and wedges of lime for squeezing over on the side. (The flavour is even better if served the next day.)

CAULIFLOWER & SPINACH CURRY

This has a coconutty red lentil sauce at its heart, while cauliflower florets and spinach are added shortly before serving to ensure they retain a bit of bite and their nutritional value. Panch phoran is a spice blend typically made up of a fragrant combination of fenugreek, fennel seeds, nigella seeds, cumin and black mustard seeds. Being a whole spice mix, it works particularly well in a slow cooker, but you could double the quantity of garam masala instead.

1 tbsp panch phoran
1 tbsp coconut oil
1 large onion, grated
1 thumb-sized piece
    of fresh root ginger,
    grated
4 large garlic cloves,
    finely grated
100 g/½ cup plus
    1 tbsp split red
    lentils, rinsed well
400 ml/1¾ cups just-
    boiled water from
    the kettle
2 tbsp tomato purée/
    paste
1 tsp ground turmeric
6 cardamom pods,
    split
1 x 400-g/14-oz. can
    coconut milk
375 g/13 oz. cauliflower
    florets
2 tsp garam masala
150 g/5 oz. baby
    spinach leaves

freshly squeezed juice
    of ½ lemon or lime
1 handful of
    coriander/cilantro
    leaves
sea salt and freshly
    ground black
    pepper
cooked brown basmati
    rice, to serve

Low 4–5 hours
High 3–4 hours

Serves 4

Toast the panch phoran in a dry frying pan/skillet over a medium-low heat for 1 minute, until they start to smell aromatic. Tip into a bowl and set aside.

Heat the coconut oil in the frying pan/skillet and add the onion, ginger and garlic and fry, stirring, for 5 minutes, until starting to colour. Transfer to the slow cooker pot with the lentils, hot water, tomato purée/paste, turmeric, cardamom and coconut. Season with salt and pepper. Cover and cook for 4–5 hours on low or 3–4 hours on high.

Forty-five minutes before the end of the cooking time, press the cauliflower florets into the sauce, making sure they are submerged as much as possible. After 30 minutes, quickly stir in the garam masala, spinach and lemon or lime juice and cook for another 15 minutes, until the cauliflower is tender and the spinach has wilted. Season with salt and pepper, to taste and serve with brown basmati rice, sprinkled with coriander/cilantro leaves.

SWEET POTATO & PEANUT CURRY

The peanut butter adds a rich creaminess to this curry – try to buy a good quality one that avoids palm oil and sugar and uses the whole nut. Peanuts are an excellent source of plant-based protein as well as numerous vitamins and minerals, while sweet potatoes provide fibre, beta carotene and vitamin C, a combination of ingredients that culminates in a satisfying filling main course or side dish.

1 tbsp coconut oil

1 onion, finely chopped

1 thumb-sized piece of fresh root ginger, coarsely grated

3 garlic cloves, finely chopped

1 medium-hot red chilli/chile, sliced, plus extra to serve

1½ tsp brown mustard seeds

2 sprigs of curry leaves

1 star anise

670 g/1 lb. 8 oz. sweet potatoes, peeled, sliced and cut into 2-cm/1-in. chunks

400-g/14-oz. can cherry tomatoes

300 ml/1¼ cups just-boiled water from the kettle

2 rounded tbsp whole-nut peanut butter (no added sugar)

freshly squeezed juice of ½ lime

1 handful of roughly chopped coriander/cilantro leaves

4 tbsp roasted unsalted peanuts, roughly chopped

sea salt and freshly ground black pepper

TO SERVE

warmed wholemeal chapattis

lime wedges

Low 3–3½ hours

High 2½–3 hours

Serves 4

Heat the coconut oil in a frying pan/skillet over a medium heat. Add the onion and fry for 6 minutes, until starting to soften. Turn the heat down slightly, add the ginger, garlic, chilli/chile and spices and cook for another minute, stirring.

Transfer the onion mix to the slow cooker pot with the sweet potatoes, canned tomatoes and hot water, then stir until combined. Cover and cook for 3–3½ hours on low or 2½–3 hours on high, until the sweet potato is tender and starts to break down in places. Turn off the heat, stir in the peanut butter and lime juice, without breaking down the sweet potato too much, then season with salt and pepper to taste. Leave to sit for 5 minutes to heat through.

Serve topped with the coriander/cilantro, peanuts and extra chilli/chile, with the chapattis on the side for scooping up the sauce and lime wedges for squeezing.

CHANA MASALA

Made with everyday store cupboard ingredients, this popular chickpea/garbanzo bean curry requires little effort – apart from frying the onion, you pretty much bung everything into the pot and let it bubble away. Spices are well known for the positive effect they have in supporting our gut health, while ginger is a superstar when it comes to aiding digestion.

2 tsp cumin seeds

2 tbsp ghee or coconut oil

1 onion, finely chopped

4 garlic cloves, finely chopped

1 thumb-sized piece of fresh root ginger, finely grated

1½ x 400-g/14-oz. cans chickpeas/garbanzo beans (or 150 g/¾ cup plus 3 tbsp dried chickpeas, soaked overnight and cooked), drained (reserve 70 ml/scant ⅓ cup of the chickpea water or aquafaba)

1 x 400-g/14-oz. can chopped tomatoes

½ tsp dried chilli/hot pepper flakes

1 tsp ground turmeric

1½ tsp ground coriander

1 tsp garam masala

freshly squeezed juice of ½ lemon or 1 tsp tamarind paste

125 g/4 oz. baby spinach leaves

sea salt and freshly ground black pepper

TO SERVE

4 heaped tbsp thick natural/plain yogurt, or dairy-free alternative

1 handful of coriander/cilantro leaves

½ red onion, thinly sliced into rings

warmed flatbreads, to serve (optional)

Low 4–5 hours
High 3–4 hours

Serves 4

Toast the cumin seeds in a dry frying pan/skillet for 2 minutes, tossing the pan/skillet occasionally, until they smell aromatic. Tip into a bowl and set aside.

Heat the ghee or oil in the frying pan/skillet over a medium heat and fry the onion for 6 minutes, until softened. Add the garlic and ginger and cook for another 2 minutes, stirring. Tip the onion mixture into the slow cooker pot with three-quarters of the toasted cumin.

Add the chickpeas/garbanzo beans, aquafaba, chopped tomatoes, chilli/hot pepper flakes and turmeric. Cover and cook for 4–5 hours on low or 3–4 hours on high. Twenty minutes before the curry is ready, add the ground coriander, garam masala, lemon juice or tamarind and spinach. Stir until combined, then cover and finish cooking.

Serve topped with a spoonful of yogurt, coriander/cilantro, slices of red onion and sprinkled with the remaining cumin, with flatbreads on the side.

ETHIOPIAN RED LENTIL BERBERE

Berbere is a fragrant Ethiopian spice blend based on chilli/chile, ginger, fenugreek, paprika, cumin, garlic, cardamom, coriander/cilantro and nigella, which work together to give an unmistakeable depth of flavour, alongside being antiviral and antibacterial. This curry is traditionally served with injera, a thin fermented pancake made from teff flour, if you can't find them, flatbreads or chapattis would be a good alternative.

30 g/2 tbsp butter or dairy-free alternative
1 large onion, finely chopped
3 garlic cloves, finely chopped
1 thumb-sized piece of fresh root ginger, coarsely grated
2 tbsp tomato purée/paste
350 g/12 oz. vine-ripened tomatoes, chopped
225 g/1¼ cups split red lentils, rinsed well
4 tsp berbere spice blend
2 bay leaves
850 ml/3⅔ cups hot vegetable stock/broth
125 g/4 oz. baby spinach leaves
freshly squeezed juice of ½ lemon, plus wedges of lemon
sea salt and freshly ground black pepper

TO SERVE
6 tbsp thick natural/plain yogurt or dairy-free alternative
injera or wholewheat flatbreads or chapatti

Low 3½–4½ hours
High 2½–3½ hours

Serves 4

Heat the butter in a frying pan/skillet over a medium heat. Add the onion and cook for 7 minutes, until softened. Add the garlic and ginger and cook for 2 minutes, stirring.

Transfer the onion mix to the slow cooker pot and add the tomato purée/paste, fresh tomatoes, half the berbere spice blend, bay leaves and hot stock/broth. Stir until combined. Cover and cook for 3½ –4½ hours on low or 2½–3½ hours on high, until the lentils are tender.

Fifteen minutes before the end of the cooking time, stir in the remaining spice blend, the spinach and lemon juice. Add a splash of hot water if the curry looks very dry. Season well with salt and pepper to taste. Serve topped with a spoonful of yogurt, injera or flatbreads and lemon wedges for squeezing over.

BUNNY CHOW

This meat-free version of the popular Durban street-food curry is served in a hollowed-out bread roll or loaf. The traditional way to eat it is to tear off chunks of the bread and use to scoop up the curry inside. Don't be put off by the long list of spices – they work harmoniously together to create a rich, deeply flavoured curry that is easy to make.

1 cinnamon stick
1 star anise
½ tsp fennel seeds
1½ tsp cumin seeds
1½ tsp coriander
   seeds
seeds from
   6 cardamom pods
1 onion, grated
1 thumb-sized piece
   of fresh root ginger,
   grated
4 garlic cloves, grated
1 tsp ground turmeric
10 curry leaves
2 bay leaves
1 tbsp coconut oil
2 tbsp tomato purée/
   paste
400 g/14 oz. potatoes,
   peeled and cut into
   2-cm/1-in. chunks
2 carrots, halved
   lengthways and cut
   into 1-cm/½-in.
   chunks

1 x 400-g/14-oz. can
   kidney beans,
   drained
500 ml/2 cups hot
   vegetable stock/
   broth
½ red onion, thinly
   sliced into rings
freshly squeezed juice
   of 1 lime
sea salt and freshly
   ground black
   pepper
crusty bread rolls, to
   serve
oil, for brushing

Low 5–6 hours
High 4–5 hours

Serves 4

Put the cinnamon, star anise, fennel seeds, cumin seeds, coriander seeds and cardamom seeds in a large, dry frying pan/skillet over a medium-low heat and toast for 1–2 minutes, until they start to smell aromatic. Leave to cool, then grind in a grinder or using a pestle and mortar.

Put the rest of the ingredients up to and excluding the red onion into the slow cooker pot and stir until combined. Cover and cook for 5–6 hours on low or 4–5 hours on high.

Meanwhile, prepare the rolls. You can either serve the rolls as is or crisp them up in the oven before filling with the curry. Brush all over with oil and bake in an oven preheated to 200°C/400°F/Gas 6 for 5 minutes, until crisp. Cut off the top of each roll to make a lid and scoop out the centre – you can save these to make breadcrumbs.

Toss the red onion in the juice of ½ lime and season with salt, then set aside.

When the curry is ready, add the rest of the lime juice and season with salt and pepper to taste. Spoon the curry into the hollowed-out rolls and serve topped with a few red onions.

SRI LANKAN MUNG BEAN DAHL

In Ayurveda, mung beans are held in high esteem and considered the queen of legumes. They are said to have the highest nutritional value of all legumes, being rich in fibre, protein and certain minerals as well as easy to digest – what's more they don't require pre-soaking, which adds to the simplicity of this comforting, sustaining dahl.

220 g/1¼ cups split mung beans, rinsed well
1 tsp ground turmeric
5 curry leaves
850 ml/3½ cups just-boiled water from the kettle
100 g/3½ oz. baby spinach leaves
15 g/1 tbsp butter or dairy-free alternative
freshly squeezed juice of ½ lemon
sea salt and freshly ground black pepper
chapatti or naan and Red Onion Pickle (page 115), to serve (optional)

TARKA
25 g/1½ tbsp plus 1 tsp butter or dairy-free alternative
1 onion, diced
3 garlic cloves, finely chopped
½ tsp cumin seeds
½ tsp dried chilli/hot pepper flakes
½ tsp brown mustard seeds

Low 4–5 hours
High 3–4 hours

Serves 4

Put the mung beans, turmeric and curry leaves in the slow-cooker pot and pour in the just-boiled water. Cover with the lid and cook for 4–5 hours on low or 3–4 hours on high, until the mung beans are tender and start to break down.

Ten minutes before the end of the cooking time, quickly stir in the spinach and season the dahl generously with salt and pepper. Add a splash more hot water if you feel it's needed. Continue to cook until the spinach wilts, then turn off the heat and stir in the butter and lemon juice.

Meanwhile, make the tarka. Melt the butter in a small frying pan/skillet over a medium heat. Add the onion and fry for 8 minutes, until softened. Turn down the heat slightly and stir in the garlic, cumin seeds, chilli/hot pepper flakes and mustards seeds and cook for another 2 minutes, until the garlic just starts to turn golden – you want it to have a slightly toasted flavour but not burn.

Spoon the tarka over the dahl and serve with chapatti or naan by the side for scooping up the dahl. It's also good with the red onion pickle, if you like.

YELLOW SPLIT PEA DAHL WITH TOMATO TARKA

Like red lentils, yellow split peas cook down into a comforting thick dahl when cooked low 'n' slow. The tomatoes not only add a burst of flavour and colour, cooking them in ghee or butter enhances the availability of lycopene. This antioxidant helps protect the health of the eyes and gut. Serve with warm wholewheat chapattis.

300 g/1⅓ cups yellow split peas, soaked for 1 hour, drained and rinsed well
1½ tsp ground turmeric
2 bay leaves
700 ml/24 fl. oz. just-boiled water from the kettle
freshly squeezed juice of ½ lemon
sea salt and freshly ground black pepper
1 handful of chopped coriander/cilantro leaves, to garnish

TOMATO TARKA
50 g/3½ tbsp ghee, butter or dairy-free alternative
2 tsp cumin seeds
4 large garlic cloves, finely chopped
½–1 tsp dried chilli/hot pepper flakes
1½ tsp brown mustard seeds
350 g/12⅓ oz. mixed vine-ripened tomatoes, deseeded if large, roughly chopped

Low 5–6 hours
High 4–5 hours

Serves 4

Put the split peas into the slow cooker pot, add the turmeric, bay leaves and pour over the just-boiled water to cover, then stir until combined. Cover and cook for 5–6 hours on low or for 4–5 hours on high, until the split peas are tender and start to break down. Season generously with salt and stir in the lemon juice.

Just before the split peas are ready, make the tomato tarka. Heat the ghee in a small frying pan/skillet over a medium-low heat. Stir in the cumin, garlic, chilli/hot pepper flakes and mustard seeds and fry for 2 minutes, stirring, until the seeds smell toasted and the garlic starts to change colour. Add the tomatoes and cook for another 3 minutes, until they start to break down. Season with salt and pepper.

Spoon the split pea dahl into a serving bowl and top with the tomatoes and coriander/cilantro.

STEWS & HOT POTS

BLACK BEAN, SQUASH & SWEETCORN/CORN POT

Both hearty and sustaining, this lightly spiced one-pot meal provides healthy amounts of quality carbs, fibre, protein and good fats. Serve it on its own, topped with sliced avocado or with quinoa as a side. If in season, use fresh corn on the cob, alternatively canned or frozen make a convenient swap – just make sure you defrost it first.

150 g/1 cup dried black beans, soaked overnight
1 tbsp cumin seeds
1 tbsp coriander seeds
1 tbsp extra-virgin olive oil
1 onion, finely chopped
3 garlic cloves, finely chopped
1 red (bell) pepper, deseeded and cut into 1-cm/½-in. dice
1 medium-hot red chilli/chile, sliced
475 g/1 lb. 1 oz. peeled and deseeded squash, cut into 2-cm/1-in. chunks
400 ml/1¾ cups just-boiled water from the kettle

1 x 400-g/14-oz. can chopped tomatoes
1 handful of thyme stems, or 1½ tsp dried
2 sweetcorn, kernels sliced off the cob (about 200 g/7 oz.)
1 rounded tsp vegetable bouillon powder
juice of 1 lime, freshly squeezed
sea salt and freshly ground black pepper
coriander/cilantro leaves, to garnish
cooked quinoa, to serve (optional)

Low 6–7 hours
High 5–6 hours

Serves 4

Drain and rinse the soaked beans then put them in a saucepan. Cover with plenty of cold water and bring to the boil, then leave to bubble away for 10 minutes. Turn the heat down slightly and simmer for another 10 minutes, then drain and tip into the slow cooker pot.

Meanwhile, toast the cumin and coriander seeds in a dry frying pan/skillet over a medium-low heat for 1–2 minutes, until they start to smell aromatic. Leave to cool, then grind in a grinder or using a pestle and mortar.

Add the ground spices to the slow cooker pot with the rest of the ingredients up to and excluding the sweetcorn. Stir until combined then cook for 6–7 hours on low or for 5–6 hours on high. Thirty minutes before the end of the cooking time, quickly stir in the sweetcorn and vegetable bouillon so you don't lose too much heat from the pot. Cover and cook until the sweetcorn is just tender – I quite like it with a bit of bite in contrast to the soft squash and beans.

Season with lime juice and salt and pepper to taste and served sprinkled with coriander/cilantro. Serve with quinoa, if you like.

MUSHROOM & BROWN LENTIL RAGU

Deep, earthy, flavourful, filling… what's not to like about this hearty meat-free ragù? The portion size is on the generous side but, like most ragùs and sauces of this type, they almost taste better the next day so it's worth making a larger quantity for subsequent meals. It comes served with tagliatelle or pappardelle, but I also like the ragù with polenta.

30 g/1 cup dried porcini mushrooms
3 tbsp extra-virgin olive oil
1 large onion, finely chopped
1 celery stick/rib, finely chopped
1 carrot, finely diced
4 garlic cloves, finely chopped
380 g/13 oz. chestnut mushrooms, roughly chopped
150 ml/²/₃ cup red wine or extra hot stock/broth
about 300 ml/1¼ cups hot vegetable stock/broth
160 g/1 cup brown lentils, rinsed

400 g/14 oz. passata
1 tsp dried thyme
2 bay leaves
1 tsp yeast extract or brown barley miso
salt and freshly ground black pepper

TO SERVE
cooked tagliatelle or pappardelle pasta
grated vegetarian Parmesan (optional)
freshly chopped basil

Low 6–7 hours
High 4½–5½ hours

Serves 4

Put the dried porcini in a heatproof bowl and pour over enough just-boiled water to cover. Leave to rehydrate for 30 minutes. Strain the mushrooms over a bowl with a slotted spoon and squeeze out any excess liquid. Finely chop the porcini and set aside.

Meanwhile, heat the olive oil in a large frying pan/skillet over a medium heat and fry the onion, celery and carrot for 5 minutes, until starting to soften. Add the garlic, rehydrated porcini and chestnut mushrooms and cook, stirring often, for another 5 minutes, until softened.

Pour the red wine into the pan, if using, and allow to boil until reduced and there is no aroma of alcohol – alternatively leave this step out and increase the quantity of hot stock/broth.

Pour enough hot stock/broth into the jug/pitcher containing the porcini soaking liquor to make 500 ml/2 cups. Add to the slow cooker pot with the lentils, passata and thyme and stir until combined. Add the mushroom mixture and bay leaves. Cover and cook for 6–7 hours on low or 4½–5½ hours on high. Just before the ragù is ready, stir in the yeast extract or miso and season with salt and pepper to taste, then leave to rest for 5 minutes.

Serve spooned over pasta, adding a ladleful of the pasta cooking water to the ragù, topped with grated Parmesan, if you like.

PORCINI & CELERIAC STEW WITH HERB DUMPLINGS

Dried porcini lend a real depth of flavour to the sauce of this hearty winter stew – a little goes a long way for flavour. They are joined by fresh mushrooms and root vegetables for a fibre boost. Mushrooms have prebiotic properties, supporting growth of healthy bacteria in the gut and are a source of vitamin D. Serve with steamed shredded spring greens.

15 g/½ cup dried porcini mushrooms
150 ml/⅔ cup just-boiled water from the kettle
2 tbsp extra-virgin olive oil
1 large onion, finely chopped
2 large garlic cloves, finely chopped
350 g/12 oz. chestnut mushrooms, quartered or cut into sixths if large
400 g/14 oz. celeriac, peeled and cut into 2-cm/1-in. chunks
1 large carrot, halved lengthways and cut into 2-cm/1-in. chunks
1 celery stick/rib, finely diced
about 350 ml/1½ cups hot vegetable stock/broth
1 tbsp tomato purée/paste
2 tsp paprika
1 handful of thyme sprigs
2 bay leaves
2 tbsp soured cream or oat cream
sea salt and freshly ground black pepper

HERB DUMPLINGS
170 g/1¼ cups self-raising/rising flour, plus 1 tbsp for thickening
⅓ tsp sea salt
90 g/6 tbsp butter or dairy-free alternative
1 tbsp thyme leaves or ½ tsp dried thyme
about 1½ tbsp milk of choice or water

Low 6½–7½ hours
High 4½–5½ hours

Serves 4

Put the porcini in a small heatproof bowl and cover with the boiled water. Top with a plate and leave to rehydrate for 20 minutes. Strain, reserving the soaking water in a measuring jug/pitcher and squeezing the porcini of any excess water. Finely chop and set aside. While the porcini is soaking, heat the olive oil in a deep frying pan/skillet and fry the onion for 5 minutes. Add the garlic, chestnut mushrooms and chopped porcini and cook, stirring often, for 5 minutes. Stir in 1 tablespoon flour and cook for 1 minute to thicken the sauce. Tip the mushroom mixture into the slow cooker pot and add the celeriac, carrot and celery. Pour enough hot vegetable stock/broth into the jug/pitcher containing the porcini soaking water to make 550 ml/2⅓ cups. Stir in the tomato purée/paste and paprika. Pour the liquid into the slow cooker pot, covering the vegetables. Add the thyme sprigs and bay leaves. Cover and cook for 6½–7½ hours on low or 4½–5½ hours on high.

For the herb dumplings, 1½ hours before the end of the cooking time, mix the flour and salt together in a bowl. Rub the butter in with your fingertips, then stir in the thyme and the milk/water until it comes together into a ball; make sure it's not too wet. Form the dough into 12 ping pong-sized balls. Stir your cream into the stew and season with salt and pepper. Place the dumplings, evenly spaced out, on top of the stew, pressing down so they are half submerged in the sauce. Cover and cook on high for 1–1¼ hours until risen and fluffy. Serve the stew with 3 dumplings per person.

BLACK EYE PEA STEW WITH ALLSPICE

Jamaican in feel thanks to the combination of thyme, allspice, turmeric and Scotch bonnet chilli/chile, this substantial stew is topped with light and fluffy cornmeal dumplings. All that is needed to make a complete meal is some steamed leafy greens.

1 tbsp coconut oil

1 large onion, finely chopped

1 red (bell) pepper, deseeded and cut into 2-cm/1-in. pieces

1 large carrot, quartered lengthways and cut into 1-cm/½-in. chunks

3 garlic cloves, finely chopped

650 g/1 lb. 7 oz. butternut squash, peeled, deseeded and cut into 2-cm/ 1-in. chunks

1½ tbsp thyme leaves or 1½ tsp dried thyme

¾ tsp ground allspice

1 tsp ground turmeric

1 Scotch bonnet chilli/ chile, left whole

600 ml/2½ cups hot vegetable stock/broth

1½ x 400-g/14-oz. can black eye peas, drained

sea salt and freshly ground black pepper

CORNMEAL DUMPLINGS

100 g/¾ cup plain/ all-purpose flour

100 g/⅔ cup coarse cornmeal

1 tsp baking powder

½ tsp salt, plus extra for seasoning

75 g/⅓ cup butter or dairy-free alternative

1 egg, lightly beaten

Low 4–5 hours
High 3–4 hours

Serves 4

Heat the coconut oil in a large frying pan/skillet over a medium heat. Add the onion, red (bell) pepper and carrot and fry for 7 minutes, until starting to soften. Add the garlic and cook for another 2 minutes, stirring.

Transfer the onion mixture to the slow cooker pot and add the squash, thyme, allspice, turmeric and Scotch bonnet. Pour in the hot stock/broth, add the black eye peas and stir until combined. Cover and cook for 4–5 hours on low of 3–4 hours on high, until the vegetables are tender.

Meanwhile, make the cornmeal dumplings. Put the flour, cornmeal, baking powder and salt in a mixing bowl and rub in the butter with your fingertips until the mixture resembles coarse breadcrumbs. Stir in the egg. Divide the mixture into eight balls, then flatten into a patty about 1-cm/½-in. thick.

Forty minutes before the end of the cooking time, season the stew with salt and pepper to taste. Place the dumplings on top of the stew, spacing them out evenly, and taking as little time as possible to ensure you don't lose too much heat from the pot. Cover and continue to cook until the dumplings are light and fluffy.

BELUGA LENTILS WITH SQUASH

With their earthy, nutty flavour, beluga are said to be the most nutritious of all the lentils providing beneficial amounts of fibre, protein, iron, calcium, potassium and B vitamins. This simple stew-of-sorts comes toppes with a spoonful of turmeric and garlic may and makes a perfect weekday meal or side dish.

2 tsp coriander seeds

2 tbsp extra-virgin olive oil

1 large onion, finely chopped

3 large garlic, finely chopped

125 g/1¼ cups black beluga lentils, rinsed

½ tsp ground turmeric

600 g/1 lb. 5 oz. butternut squash, peeled, seeds removed and cut into 2-cm/1-in. pieces

500 ml/2 cups hot vegetable stock/ broth

150 g/5 oz. baby spinach leaves

freshly squeezed juice of ½ lemon

sea salt and freshly ground black pepper

warmed flatbreads, to serve

TURMERIC & GARLIC MAYO

6 tbsp good-quality mayonnaise or vegan alternative

1 garlic clove, crushed

½ tsp ground turmeric

squeeze of lemon juice

freshly ground black pepper

Low 2½–3½ hours
High 1½–2½ hours

Serves 4–6

Toast the coriander seeds in a large, dry frying pan/skillet for 2 minutes, until they smell aromatic. Tip the seeds into a bowl and set aside. Heat the olive oil in the pan over a medium heat, add the onion and fry for 7 minutes, until softened. Add the garlic and cook for another 2 minutes, stirring.

Tip the lentils, turmeric and squash into the pan and stir until combined, then transfer to the slow cooker pot with the hot stock/broth and half the toasted coriander seeds. Cover with the lid and cook for 2½–3½ hours on low or 1½–2½ hours on high, until the lentils and squash are tender.

Fifteen minutes before the end of the cooking time, quickly stir in the spinach, lemon juice and remaining coriander seeds. Cover and continue to cook until the spinach wilts. Season with salt and pepper to taste. Spoon into shallow bowls and serve topped with a spoonful of the turmeric and garlic mayo and flatbreads on the side.

Turmeric & Garlic Mayo: Combining all the ingredients in a bowl and mixing to blend. Cover and refrigerate until ready to serve.

RED PEPPER, CHICKPEA & HARISSA STEW

Perfect served with warm crusty bread for mopping up the juices, this simple store cupboard stew needs little in the way of adornment. A jar of the North African spice paste, harissa, is a permanent feature in my kitchen as it's a convenient and easy way to add flavour to everything from rice and grain dishes to soups, marinades and stews, as here.

2 tsp cumin seeds

3 tbsp extra-virgin olive oil

2 red onions, thinly sliced

2 red (bell) peppers, deseeded and cut lengthways into 1-cm/½-in. wide slices

4 garlic cloves, finely chopped

5 sprigs of thyme

400-g/14-oz. can chopped tomatoes

1 tbsp tomato purée/paste

150 ml/⅔ cup hot vegetable stock/broth

400-g/14-oz. can chickpeas/garbanzo beans, drained

2 tbsp harissa paste

2 tsp hot smoked paprika

sea salt and freshly ground black pepper

thick natural/plain yogurt, or dairy-free alternative, and lemon wedges, to serve

Low 3–4 hours
High 2–3 hours

Serves 4

Toast the cumin seeds in a large, dry frying pan/ skillet for 2 minutes over a medium-low heat, until they smell toasted. Tip into a bowl and set aside.

Turn the heat to medium. Heat the oil in the pan and fry the onions and peppers for 5 minutes, until starting to soften. Add the garlic and cook for another 2 minutes.

Transfer the onions and (bell) peppers to the slow cooker pot and add the toasted cumin seeds, thyme, chopped tomatoes, tomato purée/paste, hot stock/broth, chickpeas/garbanzo beans and harissa. Cover and cook for 3–4 hours on low or 2–3 hours on high. Quickly stir in the smoked paprika 30 minutes before the end of the cooking time.

Season with salt and pepper, to taste, and serve, hot or at room temperature, topped with a good spoonful of yogurt. Serve with wedges of lemon to squeeze over.

SICILIAN WHITE BEANS WITH FENNEL & OLIVES

This light stew reminds me of hot sunshine-filled days with its golden, saffron-infused stock/broth, loaded with fresh vegetables, olives and herbs. It's just as good served at room temperature as it is warm, so don't feel you have to eat it straight after making. I use regular white potatoes as I like the way they break down a little into the sauce, thickening it slightly, but waxy new potatoes work well too, and you can keep their skins on. Serve with orzo or crusty bread and a green salad. It's also good topped with a spoonful of the Almond Aioli (see page 141).

3 tbsp extra-virgin olive oil
1 onion, halved and thinly sliced
2 garlic cloves, thinly sliced
350 g/12 oz. white potatoes, peeled and cut into 2-cm/1-in. pieces
1 fennel bulb, halved lengthways and thinly sliced
175 g/6 oz. small vine-ripened tomatoes, halved
1 x 400-g/14-oz. can cannellini beans, drained, or 100 g/½ cup plus 1 tbsp dried beans, soaked overnight and cooked (see page 14)
90 g/1 scant cup whole pitted black kalamata olives

475 ml/2 cups hot vegetable stock/broth
pinch of saffron
1 tbsp tomato purée/paste
1 handful of thyme sprigs
2 bay leaves
200 g/7 oz. small cauliflower florets
freshly squeezed juice of ½ lemon, and lemon wedges
sea salt and freshly ground black pepper

Low 5–6 hours
High 4–5 hours

Serves 4

Heat the oil in a frying pan/skillet over a medium heat and fry the onions for 7 minutes, until softened. Add the garlic and cook for another 2 minutes.

Tip the onion and garlic into the slow cooker pot and add the potatoes, fennel, tomatoes, cannellini beans and olives. Mix together the hot stock/broth, saffron and tomato purée/paste and pour into the slow cooker pot to cover the vegetables. Tuck in the herbs. Cover with the lid and cook for 5–6 hours on low or 4–5 hours on high.

Thirty minutes before the end of the cooking time, quickly stir in the cauliflower and lemon juice, pressing the florets into the stock/broth, and making sure you don't lose too much heat in the pot. Cover and cook until the cauliflower is tender. Season with the salt and pepper to taste. Serve with orzo or crusty bread and a spoonful of almond aioli, if you like.

BIG BOWL CHILLI

Tempeh almost becomes mince-/ground meat-like when crumbled and readily takes on the flavour of what it's served with, so it's perfect for a veggie chilli/chili where there are lots of big, bold flavours. I've gone for borlotti, instead of the more usual red kidney beans, while the sweet potato adds a splash of colour. While you can't really taste the coffee, it gives a depth of flavour to the chilli/chile as well as rich colour.

2 tbsp extra-virgin olive oil

1 large onion, diced

3 garlic cloves, finely chopped

200 g/1¾ cups tempeh, crumbled

400-g/14-oz. can borlotti beans, drained

6 cloves

2 bay leaves

200 ml/¾ cup hot strong coffee

400-g/14-oz. can chopped tomatoes

½ tsp dried chilli/hot pepper flakes

1 tbsp tomato purée/paste

1 tbsp chipotle paste

2 tsp dried oregano

½ tsp light soft brown sugar

325 g/11 oz. sweet potatoes, peeled and cut into 2-cm/1-in. chunks

1 tsp ground cumin

1 tsp ground coriander

freshly squeezed juice of 1 lime, and wedges to serve

1 handful of chopped coriander/cilantro

sea salt and freshly ground black pepper

4 tbsp soured cream or dairy-free alternative, to serve

Low 5–6 hours
High 4–5 hours

Serves 4

Heat the olive oil in a large frying pan/skillet over a medium heat, add the onion and cook for 7 minutes, until softened. Add the garlic and cook for 2 minutes, stirring.

Transfer the onion mixture to the slow cooker pot and add the tempeh, beans, cloves, bay leaves, hot coffee, chopped tomatoes, chilli/hot pepper flakes, tomato purée/paste, chipotle paste, oregano, sugar and sweet potatoes, then stir until combined, pressing the sweet potatoes down under the liquid.

Cover and cook for 5–6 hours on low or 4–5 hours on high, until the sweet potatoes are tender. Thirty minutes before the end of the cooking time, stir in the cumin and ground coriander and season with salt and pepper, to taste. Add the lime juice and serve in shallow bowls, topped with coriander/cilantro and a spoonful of soured cream.

WINTER ROOT & HERB HOTPOT

A hug in a bowl... this is packed with root vegetables, winter herbs, peas, beans and barley. It makes use of a soup mix, a ready-made mixture of dried beans, grains and lentils, and a convenient and economical way to buy without having to invest in lots of separate bags. (I tend to avoid the ones with large marrowfat peas as they seem to take an age to soften!) Save the carrot and parsnip peelings to turn into nutritious, fibre-full crisps/chips to scatter over the hotpot at the end. Along with carrot and parsnip, potato and beetroot skins are equally good.

2 tbsp extra-virgin olive oil, plus extra to serve
1 onion, chopped
2 garlic cloves, finely chopped
2 celery sticks/ribs, diced
2 carrots, quartered lengthways and cut into 2-cm/1-in. chunks
1 turnip/rutabaga, sliced and cut into 2-cm/1-in. chunks
1 parsnip, sliced and cut into 2-cm/1-in. chunks
100 g/²⁄₃ cup pea and barley soup mix (or your favourite soup mix)
2 bay leaves
5 thyme sprigs
1 tbsp finely chopped rosemary

1–1.2 litres/4–5 cups hot vegetable stock/broth
2 tbsp tomato purée/paste
1 tsp cornflour/cornstarch (optional)
sea salt and freshly ground black pepper

CARROT & PARSNIP CRISPS
carrot and parsnips, skin pared into long, thin ribbons
olive oil
sea salt

Low 6–7 hours
High 5–6 hours

Serves 4

Heat the olive oil in a large frying pan/skillet over a medium heat. Add the onion and fry for 7 minutes, until softened. Add the garlic and cook for another 2 minutes, stirring.

Transfer the onion mix to the slow cooker pot with the celery, root vegetables, soup mix, herbs, the smaller quantity of hot stock/broth and tomato purée/paste, then stir until combined. Cover and cook for 6–7 hours on low or 5–6 hours on high, until the vegetables and soup mix are tender, adding more hot stock/broth if needed.

If the stew needs thickening, 5 minutes before the end of the cooking time, mix the cornflour/cornstarch with a little cold water, then stir well into the slow cooker pot. Cover and continue to cook until thickened. Season to taste and serve in bowls, topped with an extra splash of olive oil and the carrot and parsnip crisps/chips (see below).

Carrot & Parsnip Crisps: Preheat the oven to 180°C/350°F/Gas 4. Place the vegetable peelings on a large baking sheet. Drizzle over a little olive oil and toss with your hands until the peelings are lightly coated in oil. Spread them out, making sure they are not overcrowded. Season with salt. Bake in the preheated oven for 25 minutes, turning once or twice, until golden and crisp. Drain the on kitchen paper/paper towels and leave to cool and crisp up further before serving.

KOREAN-BRAISED TOFU POT

Gently slow-cooking tofu in a flavoursome Korean-style broth is the perfect way to imbibe it with plenty of flavour. Before you do anything, it's essential to remove as much excess liquid as possible from the tofu to avoid diluting the taste of the broth, so take time to drain and pat it dry. Tofu is one of a few plant-based complete proteins, meaning it provides all nine of the essential amino acids required for the repair and maintenance of our bodies, including immunity. Served on a bed of noodles, it is equally good with brown jasmine rice.

550 ml/2¼ cups just-boiled water from the kettle

2 tbsp gochujang paste

1½ tbsp soy sauce

2 tsp sesame oil

½ tsp light soft brown sugar

2 large garlic cloves, thinly sliced

1 thumb-sized piece of fresh root ginger, thickly sliced into rounds

2 spring onions/scallions, white and green parts separated, thinly sliced diagonally

450 g/1 lb. firm tofu, drained and patted dry, cut into 1-cm/½-in. thick slices

freshly ground black pepper

TO SERVE

about 400 g/2 cups cooked egg or brown rice noodles

2 tsp toasted sesame seeds

1 handful of Thai or regular basil

1 tsp dulse or nori dried seaweed flakes (optional)

4 pak choi, halved and steamed

Low 2–3 hours
High 1½–2 hours

Serves 4

Pour the hot water into the slow cooker pot and mix in the gochujang paste, soy sauce, sesame oil, sugar, garlic, ginger and white part of the spring onions/scallions, then season with pepper.

Add the tofu and spoon the sauce over until coated, pressing the tofu down into the liquid so it is submerged as much as possible. Cover and cook for 2–3 hours on low or 1½–2 hours on high, until the broth infuses the tofu with flavour. It will also darken in colour.

Divide the noodles between four large shallow bowls. Using a slotted spoon or spatula, scoop out the tofu, taking care not to break the slices, and arrange on top of the noodles. Pick the ginger out of the broth and ladle it over the noodles and tofu.

Serve topped with the sesame seeds, basil, green part of the spring onions/scallions and seaweed, if using. Arrange the pak choi to the side of the bowl. Serve straightaway.

GREEK-STYLE BUTTER BEANS WITH FETA

Shake off any preconceptions you may have about butter/lima beans, here they come in a richly flavoured tomato sauce with a slight hit of fresh chilli/chile. This dish can be served as a main meal with the carb of your choice and a green salad, or as a side.

4 tbsp extra-virgin olive oil, plus extra to serve
2 red onions, halved and sliced
2 carrots, diced
1 celery stick/rib, diced
4 garlic cloves, finely chopped
50 g/½ cup minus ½ tbsp sun-dried tomatoes in oil, drained and roughly chopped
200 g/7 oz. (about 20) small tomatoes on the vine, halved, vine reserved
1 medium-hot red chilli/chile, deseeded and thinly sliced diagonally
2 x 400-g/14-oz. cans butter/lima beans
2 tbsp tomato purée/paste
1 tbsp fresh thyme

150 ml/²⁄₃ cup hot vegetable stock/broth
2 bay leaves
freshly squeezed juice of 1 small lemon
200 g/7 oz. feta, crumbled, or dairy-free alternative
1 handful of mint leaves
sea salt and freshly ground black pepper
flatbreads or bulghur wheat, to serve

Low 3–4 hours
High 2–3 hours

Serves 4

Heat the oil in a large frying pan/skillet over a medium heat and fry the onions, carrots and celery for 8 minutes, until starting to soften but not colour. Turn the heat down slightly and add the garlic and cook for another 2 minutes, stirring, then tip everything into the slow cooker pot.

Add the sun-dried tomatoes, tomatoes, chilli/chile, butter/lima beans, tomato purée/paste, thyme and hot stock/broth. Season with salt and pepper and stir until combined. Tuck in the bay leaves and reserved tomato vine and add half the lemon juice. Cover and cook for 3–4 hours on low or 2–3 hours on high, until the tomatoes have collapsed and the vegetables and beans are tender. Check the seasoning and add more salt and pepper, if needed.

Squeeze over the remaining lemon juice and top with the crumbled feta and mint leaves. Serve warm or at room temperature with flatbreads or bulghur wheat.

SPANISH PISTO

Reminiscent of the French ratatouille, this Spanish version is flavoured with smoked paprika and a splash of red wine vinegar. Loaded with veg, it's equally delicious served hot as it is at room temperature, as a main meal with bulghur wheat or rice or as a side. I'd recommend topping it with a good spoonful or two of picada, a zesty, crunchy, nutty, herby accompaniment for the finishing touch.

4 tbsp extra-virgin olive oil

1 large onion, chopped

2 aubergines/eggplants, cut into 2-cm/1-in. chunks

3 garlic cloves, finely chopped

2 courgettes/zucchini, halved lengthways and cut into 1-cm/½-in. chunks

1½ tsp dried thyme

2 tsp smoked paprika

250 g/8¾ oz. roasted red peppers from a jar, drained and rinsed if in vinegar, roughly chopped

2 x 400-g/14-oz. cans good-quality whole plum tomatoes, roughly chopped

1 medium-hot red chilli/chile, thinly sliced

1 tsp red wine vinegar or freshly squeezed lemon juice

sea salt and freshly ground black pepper

Picada, to serve (see page 141) (optional)

Low 4–5 hours
High 3–4 hours

Serves 4–6

Heat the oil in a large frying pan/skillet over a medium heat and fry the onion and aubergine/eggplant for 10 minutes, until softened and starting to colour. Add the garlic and sauté for another 2 minutes.

Tip the oil, onion and aubergine/eggplant into the slow cooker pot with the rest of the ingredients up to and excluding the vinegar. Cover and cook for 4–5 hours on low or 3–4 hours on high. Stir in the vinegar or lemon juice and season with salt and pepper to taste. Serve with a generous spoonful of the picada.

BIG VEG DISHES

BARLEY ORZOTTO WITH BUTTERY GREENS & WALNUTS

The beauty of this risotto-of-sorts is that is doesn't require looking after and can simply be left to do its own thing. Barley is preferable to the more usual arborio rice as it holds its shape in a slow cooker, but still has a creamy texture. Brown rice miso adds both a deep umami flavour and rich colour. The miso is best added towards the end of the cooking time, so it retains its nutritional value and probiotic properties. This makes a filling, heart-warming meal.

1 tbsp extra-virgin olive oil

1 celery stick/rib, finely chopped

2 large shallots, finely chopped

3 garlic cloves, finely chopped

300 g/1½ cups pearl barley, rinsed

1.2 litres/5 cups hot vegetable stock/broth

1 tbsp finely chopped rosemary or thyme

30 g/2 tbsp butter or dairy-free alternative

150 g/5 oz. cavolo nero, tough stalks removed and thinly sliced

1 tbsp brown rice miso

freshly ground black pepper

TO SERVE

60 g/½ cup walnut halves, toasted and roughly chopped

25 g/⅓ cup finely grated vegetarian Parmesan or dairy-free alternative (optional)

Low 4–5 hours
High 2½–3½ hours

Serves 4

Heat the oil in a large frying pan/skillet over a medium heat and fry the celery and shallots for 7 minutes, until softened, then add the garlic and cook for another 2 minutes.

Tip the shallot mixture into the slow cooker pot and stir in the pearl barley, hot stock/broth and herbs. Cover and cook for 4–5 hours on low or 2½–3½ hours on high.

Just before the risotto is ready, melt the butter in the frying pan/skillet over a medium heat and stir-fry the cavolo nero for 5 minutes, until wilted. Quickly stir the miso and buttery greens into the risotto until combined, then leave to sit for 5 minutes.

Serve the risotto in shallow bowls, season with plenty of black pepper and sprinkle with walnuts and Parmesan, if using.

LEVANTINE PILAF WITH POMEGRANATE & PISTACHIOS

This rice dish is fragrant with baharat seasoning, this warming spice blend is Middle Eastern in origin and typically features cumin, coriander/cilantro, cardamom, black pepper and cinnamon, although blends can vary from household to household, country to country. I've included my own blend, but you can buy it ready-made. Opt for easy-cook brown rice, since the grains retain their texture and shape in a slow cooker.

PILAF

1 tbsp extra virgin olive oil, plus extra for cooking the halloumi

1 large onion, finely chopped

3 garlic cloves, finely chopped

1 carrot, coarsely grated

250 g/heaped 1 cup easy-cook brown rice

2 tbsp Baharat Spice Mix

1 x 400-g/14-oz. can chickpeas/garbanzo beans, drained and rinsed

600 ml/2½ cups hot vegetable stock/broth

finely grated zest of 1 lemon and juice of ½ a lemon, freshly squeezed

30 g/2 tbsp butter or dairy-free alternative

sea salt and freshly ground black pepper

TO SERVE

250 g/9 oz. halloumi, patted dry and sliced (optional)

½ pomegranate, arils removed

75 g/⅔ cup pistachios, lightly toasted

2 large handfuls of chopped coriander/cilantro

BAHARAT SPICE MIX

1 tbsp coriander seeds

1 tbsp cumin seeds

10 cloves

1 tbsp black peppercorns

1 tsp cardamom seeds

2 tbsp paprika

½ tsp ground cinnamon

¼ tsp ground nutmeg

Low 2½–3½ hours
High 1½–2½ hours

Serves 4

Heat the oil in a frying pan/skillet over a medium heat and fry the onion for 7 minutes, until softened. Add the garlic and carrot and cook for another 2 minutes.

Remove from the heat, stir in the rice, baharat spice mix and chickpeas until combined then tip into the slow cooker pot. Pour over the hot stock/broth, making sure it covers the rice. Cover and cook for 2½–3½ hours on low or 1½–2½ hours on high, until the rice has absorbed the stock/broth and is tender but still retains a little bite. Just before the rice is ready, heat a splash of oil in the frying pan/skillet over a medium heat and fry the halloumi, if using, for about 2 minutes on each side until starting to turn golden.

Stir the lemon zest and juice and butter into the rice. Season to taste with salt and pepper. Spoon the rice onto a serving plate and top with the halloumi, pomegranate and pistachios. Finish with the chopped coriander/cilantro.

Baharat Spice Mix: Toast the whole spices in a large, dry frying pan/skillet for 2 minutes, tossing the pan occasionally, until they smell aromatic. Leave to cool. Tip the toasted spices into a small food processor or pestle and mortar and grind to a powder. Stir in the ground spices.

CHESTNUT, CASHEW & HERB LOAF

The is the perfect centrepiece for a meat-free Sunday lunch or main meal, served with onion gravy, roasties and lots of veg, and the beauty of it is that it takes up no oven space and requires little effort to make. A nutritious mixture of chestnuts, cashews, dried porcini and vegetables, any leftovers make a perfect sandwich filling the next day, or the loaf can be frozen for up to 3 months.

100 g/¾ cup cashew nuts
30 g/2 tbsp butter or dairy-free alternatives, plus extra for greasing
1 large onion, diced
2 celery sticks/ribs, diced
300 g/10½ oz. cups chestnut mushrooms, finely chopped
1 large carrot, coarsely grated
3 garlic cloves, finely chopped
15 g/½ cup dried porcini mushrooms
180 g/6¼ oz. pack cooked chestnuts, coarsely grated
100 g/1¾ cups wholegrain day-old breadcrumbs

1 tbsp finely chopped rosemary, plus 1 sprig
1½ tsp dried thyme
3 eggs, lightly beaten, or replace with 3 tbsp chia seeds soaked for 20 minutes in 7½ tbsp water
2 tbsp red onion chutney
sea salt and freshly ground black pepper

Low 4½–5½ hours
High 3½–4½ hours

Serves 6

Toast the cashews in a large, dry frying pan/skillet over a medium-low heat for 5 minutes, turning once, until starting to turn golden. Tip into a bowl, leave to cool, then finely chop.

Add the butter to the pan/skillet and, when melted, stir in the onion, celery, mushrooms and carrot and cook for 8 minutes, stirring, until softened. Add the garlic and cook for another 2 minutes, stirring.

Meanwhile, blitz the porcini in a mini food processor or grinder to a powder and tip into a bowl with the chestnuts, breadcrumbs, chopped rosemary, thyme, cashews and onion mixture. Season well with salt and pepper and stir until combined. Stir in the eggs or chia mix.

Grease a 900g/2 lb. loaf tin (first make sure it fits in your slow cooker pot) and tip the chestnut mixture into the tin, pressing it down evenly. Place the loaf tin in the slow cooker pot and pour in enough just-boiled water around the tin to come three-quarters up the sides.

Cover, lining the lid of the slow cooker with kitchen paper/paper towels to absorb any moisture, and cook for 4½–5½ hours on low or 3½–4½ hours on high. One hour before the end of the cooking time, spread the chutney over the top of the loaf, place the rosemary sprig on top, replenish the hot water around the tin, if needed, and replace the kitchen paper/paper towels. Continue until the loaf is cooked through when pierced with a skewer. Serve the loaf cut into slices with your favourite extras.

MOROCCAN-STUFFED PEPPERS

Couscous makes the perfect filling to soak up the flavours of the harissa, garlic, oregano, sun-dried tomato and any juice from the red peppers. Keep half an eye on the peppers towards the end of the cooking time so they keep their shape, rather than collapse.

4 red (bell) peppers
1 tbsp extra-virgin
    olive oil
1 onion, finely
    chopped
2 large garlic cloves,
    finely chopped
100 g/1 cup sun-dried
    tomatoes in oil,
    drained and finely
    chopped
1 tsp dried oregano
200 g/1¼ cups
    uncooked couscous
200 ml/¾ cup
    hot vegetable
    stock/broth

1 tbsp harissa paste
Green Herb & Chilli/
    Chile Salsa, see
    page 140 (optional)
sea salt and freshly
    ground black
    pepper
lemon wedges, for
    squeezing
coriander/cilantro, to
    garnish

Low 3–4 hours
High 2½–3 hours

Serves 4

To prepare the red (bell) peppers, slice the top off each pepper, about 1.5 cm/½-in. deep, to make a lid. Cut away the inner membrane from the main part of each (bell) pepper and pull out and discard the seedy centre.

Heat the olive oil in a frying pan/skillet over a medium heat and fry the onion for 5 minutes, until softened, then add the garlic and cook for another 2 minutes. Remove the pan from the heat and stir in the sun-dried tomatoes, oregano and couscous.

Mix together the stock/broth and harissa, pour the mixture into the pan and stir until combined. Season with salt and pepper, to taste. Spoon the couscous mixture into the red (bell) peppers, dividing it equally between each one, until almost to the top. Place the pepper lids on top.

Arrange the stuffed (bell) peppers in the slow cooker pot, packing them tightly together so they support each other. Cover with the lid and cook for 3–4 hours on low or 2½–3 hours on high, until the (bell) peppers are tender, but not too soft to collapse. Serve topped with a spoonful of the green herb and chilli/chile salsa, if you like.

SOY & SESAME AUBERGINE/EGGPLANT

I love the simplicity of this dish with the chunks of aubergine/eggplant slightly breaking down into the rich soy sesame broth. It makes an easy main dish for two people served with brown jasmine rice or noodles and steamed green veg, or as a side for four.

2 tbsp coconut oil

2 aubergines/ eggplants, cut into 1-cm/½-in. thick rounds, then bite-sized chunks

3 spring onions/ scallions, white and green parts separated, thinly sliced diagonally

2 large garlic cloves, thinly sliced

400 ml/1¾ cups just-boiled water from the kettle

1 tbsp finely grated fresh root ginger

1 heaped tsp chilli/ chile bean sauce

½ tsp light soft brown sugar (optional)

2 tbsp soy sauce

1 tsp sesame oil

60 g/heaped ½ cup roasted unsalted peanuts, roughly chopped, or 2 tsp toasted sesame seeds

1 handful of Thai or regular basil, leaves torn

freshly ground black pepper

Low 2–3 hours
High 1½–2 hours

Serves 2–4

Heat the coconut oil in a large frying pan/skillet over a medium heat and fry the aubergine/ eggplant for 6 minutes, turning occasionally, until it starts to soften and turns golden in places. Stir in the white part of the spring onions/scallions and garlic and cook for another 1 minute. Tip the aubergine/eggplant mixture into the slow cooker pot.

Mix together the hot water, ginger, chilli/chile bean sauce, sugar, if using, soy sauce and sesame oil and pour the mixture over the aubergine/ eggplant to cover, poke down any pieces of aubergine/eggplant to submerge them. Cover and cook for 2–3 hours on low or 1½–2 hours on high, until the aubergine/eggplant is tender. Season with pepper (you shouldn't need any extra salt) and serve topped with the green part of the spring onions/scallions, peanuts or sesame seeds and basil.

JACKFRUIT LETTUCE TACOS

Admittedly, I haven't always been the biggest fan of jackfruit, but steeped in this rich, smoky, almost barbecue sauce, I've been won over. That said, if preferred, you could use aubergine, mushroom or celeriac instead. For a more substantial dish, serve the tacos in warmed tortillas with steamed quinoa or bulghur wheat, the Red Onion Pickle and a red cabbage slaw on the side.

2 tsp cumin seeds
265 g/9¼ oz. passata
1 large red onion, roughly chopped
2 garlic cloves, peeled and left whole
1 tbsp extra-virgin olive oil
2 tsp chipotle chilli/chile paste
1 tsp hot smoked paprika
1 tbsp tomato ketchup
1½ tsp balsamic vinegar
500-g/1 lb 2-oz. can young jackfruit in brine, drained (270 g/9½ oz. drained weight), sliced
sea salt and freshly ground black pepper

TO SERVE
1–2 baby gem lettuces, leaves separated, or small corn tortilla wraps, warmed

200 g/scant 1 cup soured cream or dairy-free alternative
1 large avocado, halved, stone removed and diced
2 limes, cut into wedges
1 handful of coriander/cilantro leaves (optional)

FRESH RED ONION PICKLE
1 red onion, thinly sliced into rings
freshly squeezed juice of 1 orange
freshly squeezed juice of ½ lime
1 medium-hot red chilli/chile, thinly sliced, deseeded if preferred
sea salt

Low 3–4 hours
High 2–3 hours

Serves 4

Toast the cumin seeds in a dry frying pan/skillet over a medium heat for 2 minutes, tossing the pan occasionally, until they smell aromatic. Tip into a bowl and leave to cool.

Blend the passata, red onion and garlic in a blender to a purée/paste. Heat the olive oil in the frying pan/skillet, add the passata mixture and cumin and cook for 5 minutes, stirring, until reduced and thickened. Take care as the sauce can spit and splutter.

Remove the pan from the heat stir in the chipotle paste, smoked paprika, ketchup and balsamic vinegar until combined. Stir in the jackfruit and transfer to the slow cooker pot.

Cover and line the lid with kitchen paper/paper towels to absorb any moisture – you want to dry the sauce out slightly, rather than add any liquid. Cook for 3–4 hours on low or 2–3 hours on high, until the sauce has reduced, replacing the kitchen paper/paper towels halfway through if it's very wet. Stir the jackfruit when ready and spoon into a serving bowl.

Place the lettuce (or warm tortillas), soured cream, avocado, lime and coriander/cilantro leaves in separate bowls and let everyone help themselves. To serve, place a spoonful of the jackfruit and sauce in a lettuce 'cup' and top with a spoonful of the soured cream, a few pieces of avocado, a squeeze of lime and coriander/cilantro leaves, if using.

Fresh Red Onion Pickle: Mix together all the ingredients in a bowl 1 hour before you are ready to serve.

HARISSA BABY CAULIFLOWERS

Coated in a spicy harissa marinade, the baby cauliflowers are cooked on top of a bed of tomatoes and onions. If easier, replace these baby cauliflowers with large florets and reduce the cooking time by 1 hour. Serve with bulghur wheat cooked in stock/broth and a large rocket/arugula salad. Tahini is one of the most versatile of ingredients, lending a rich creaminess to cooking. The sesame seed paste also boasts impressive levels of vitamins B and E as well as the minerals, iron, magnesium and calcium.

2 tbsp rose harissa paste

1 tbsp tomato purée/paste

1 garlic clove, crushed

2 tbsp extra-virgin olive oil

2 baby cauliflowers, outer leaves removed and saved

1 red onion, halved and thinly sliced

350 g/12¼ oz. small vine-ripened tomatoes, halved

4 oregano sprigs

sea salt and freshly ground black pepper

TAHINI YOGURT

200 g/1 scant cup thick natural/plain yogurt or dairy-free alternative

2 tbsp tahini

1 garlic clove, crushed

freshly squeezed juice of ½ lemon

sea salt

Low 2½–3 hours
High 2–2½ hours

Serves 2–4

Mix together the harissa, tomato purée/paste, garlic and half the olive oil in a bowl. Season with salt and pepper.

Make a deep cross-shaped cut into the stalk of each cauliflower. Generously brush the harissa mixture over the cauliflower to coat.

Put the red onion, tomatoes, oregano sprigs, the saved cauliflower leaves, remaining olive oil and 2 tablespoons water in the slow cooker pot and stir gently until combined. Place the cauliflowers on top. Cover and cook for 2½ –3 hours on low or 2–2½ hours on high. Using a skewer, test the cauliflowers are cooked through and tender.

Serve the cauliflowers whole or cut in half if serving as a side dish, spooned on top of the tomato mixture, with a generous spoonful of the tahini yogurt.

Tahini Yogurt: Mix together all the ingredients in a small bowl. Season with salt to taste. Spoon into an airtight container and keep for up to 3 days in the fridge.

AUBERGINE/EGGPLANT PARMIGIANA

I've made many versions of this layered aubergine/eggplant, mozzarella and tomato sauce dish over the years and this slow-cooked version is definitely up there with my favourites. Slow cooking suits aubergines/eggplants, which become meltingly tender with time. I don't tend to salt them first, only if they are particularly seedy, but they definitely benefit from sautéing before being slow cooked to add colour and flavour to the final dish. Serve with crusty bread and a crisp green salad.

3 tbsp extra-virgin olive oil, plus extra for greasing
2 good-sized aubergines/eggplants, ends trimmed, cut lengthways into 1-cm/½-in. thick slices
2 x 400-g/14-oz. cans chopped tomatoes
1 tbsp tomato purée/paste
2 garlic cloves, finely chopped
1 tsp dried oregano
70 g/1¼ cups wholewheat breadcrumbs, day old
2 x 125-g/4½-oz. mozzarella balls, drained and torn into small pieces
50 g/⅔ cup finely grated vegetarian Parmesan
sea salt and freshly ground black pepper

Low 3–4 hours
High 2–3 hours

Serves 4

Heat 1 tablespoon of the olive oil in a large frying pan/skillet over a medium heat, add a third of the aubergines/eggplants and fry for 7 minutes, turning once, until softened and golden. Remove from the pan/skillet and set aside while you cook the remaining aubergines/eggplants in two batches, adding more oil when needed.

Mix together the chopped tomatoes, tomato purée/paste, garlic and oregano. Season with salt and pepper.

To assemble, brush the pot of the slow cooker with olive oil. Arrange a third of the aubergine/eggplant slices evenly over the bottom of the slow cooker pot, top with half each of the breadcrumbs and the tomato sauce. Add a half of the mozzarella and Parmesan. Arrange another third of the aubergine/eggplant slices over the top, and top with the remaining breadcrumbs and tomato sauce. Finish with a layer of the remaining aubergine/eggplant and mozzarella. Set aside the rest of the Parmesan to serve.

Cover and cook for 3–4 hours on low or for 2–3 hours on high. Turn off the heat and leave to sit for 5 minutes. If you like a golden top, cook under a hot grill/broiler until starting to bubble.

To serve, scatter over the Parmesan and serve with crusty bread and a green salad.

KIMCHI RICE

Made from fermented cabbage and other vegetables, kimchi is a simple way to add flavour and nutritional value to your cooking and comes with an impressive list of nutritional benefits. The spicy, taste bud-tickling Korean condiment is a probiotic, which improves levels of good bacteria in the gut and may also support immunity and heart health. Look for unpasteurised versions or make yourself for superior health benefits. For a vegan version, omit the egg and top with cubes of fried marinated tofu or tempeh.

250 g/1¼ cups brown jasmine rice, rinsed well

2 tbsp finely grated fresh root ginger

1 carrot, coarsely grated

4 spring onions/ scallions, white and green parts separated, thinly sliced diagonally

1 tbsp gochujang paste

1 tbsp soy sauce

600 ml/2½ cups hot vegetable stock/ broth

1 tsp sesame oil

250 g/1½ cups kimchi, roughly chopped

1 tbsp toasted sesame seeds

1 tbsp ghee or coconut oil

4 eggs (optional)

1 large handful of chopped coriander/cilantro (optional)

1 medium-hot red chilli/chile, thinly sliced (optional)

sea salt and freshly ground black pepper

Low 2–3 hours
High 1½ hours

Serves 4

Put the rice in the slow cooker pot with the ginger, carrot and the white part of the spring onions/scallions.

Mix together the gochujang paste, soy sauce and hot vegetable stock/broth and pour it over the rice. Cover and cook for 2–3 hours on low, 1½ hours on high, or until the rice is tender and the liquid has been absorbed. Stir in the sesame oil, kimchi and half the sesame seeds, replace the lid and leave to sit while you cook the eggs.

If serving the rice with an egg, heat the ghee or coconut oil in a large frying pan/skillet. Crack in the eggs, one by one, and fry until cooked to your liking.

Spoon the rice into large shallow bowls and serve topped with an egg, the green part of the spring onions/scallions, the remaining sesame seeds, coriander/cilantro and chilli/chile, if using.

PUY LENTIL, WALNUT & BLUE CHEESE SALAD

Don't feel you have to be restricted to cooking stews and hearty one-pot dishes in your slow cooker, it's more versatile than you perhaps consider. Options include bean, lentil and grain-based salads, particularly those using a combination of cooked and raw ingredients to enhance their nutritional value, colour and texture. Try to avoid serving this salad fridge-cold, it's best at room temperature or even while still warm when the cheese melts slightly in the heat of the lentils.

1 tbsp extra-virgin olive oil

1 large carrot, quartered lengthways and diced

1 celery stick/rib, diced

2 banana shallots, diced

150 g/1 scant cup Puy lentils, rinsed well

2 bay leaves

250 ml/1 cup hot vegetable stock/broth

100 g/3½ oz. watercress, spinach and rocket salad

80 g/¾ cup walnut halves, toasted and broken into pieces

100 g/½ cup vegetarian dolcelatte, or dairy-free alternative, cut into small pieces

DRESSING

2 tbsp extra-virgin olive oil

1 tbsp raw apple cider vinegar

1 tsp Dijon mustard

1 small garlic clove, crushed

sea salt and freshly ground black pepper

Low 3½–4½ hours
High 2½–3½ hours

Serves 4

Heat the olive oil in a large frying pan/skillet over a medium-low heat, add the carrot, celery and three-quarters of the diced shallot and sauté for 10 minutes, stirring occasionally, until softened.

Tip the shallot mix into the slow cooker pot and add the lentils, bay leaves and hot stock/broth – the stock/broth should just cover the lentils but not swamp them. Cover, lining the lid with kitchen paper/paper towels to absorb any moisture, and cook for 3½–4½ hours on low or 2½–3½ hours on high, until the lentils are tender and there is minimal amount of liquid in the pot. Leave to cool slightly or to room temperature.

To make the dressing, mix everything together until combined and season with salt and pepper to taste.

Spoon the lentil mixture into a large, shallow serving bowl, add the salad leaves, reserved shallot and dressing and toss until combined. Scatter over the walnuts and cheese, to serve.

SIDE DISHES & CONDIMENTS

WARM GREEN BEAN SALAD

This has a light, summery feel and would make a perfect light lunch for two served warm topped with a poached egg, crumbled cheese or chopped toasted almonds, or as a side. It's equally good served at room temperature. You could also add other summer-glut vegetables, including courgettes/zucchini, thin green beans and aubergine/eggplant for a ratatouille of sorts. Healthwise, you really can't go wrong with plentiful amounts of vegetables.

3 tbsp extra-virgin
   olive oil
4 shallots, halved and
   thinly sliced
2 large garlic cloves,
   thinly sliced
280 g/9¾ oz.
   stringless runner
   beans, cut into
   2-cm/1-in. wide
   diagonal slices
400 g/14 oz. small
   tomatoes on the
   vine, halved
   and vine saved
200 ml/¾ cup hot
   vegetable
   stock/broth

1 tbsp fresh oregano
   or 1 tsp dried
1½ tbsp tomato
   purée/paste
juice of ½ a lemon,
   freshly squeezed
1 handful of mint
   leaves
sea salt and freshly
   cracked black
   pepper

Low 2–3 hours
High 1½–2 hours

Serves 4

Heat the olive oil in a large frying pan/skillet over a medium heat and fry the shallots for 5 minutes until softened. Add the garlic and cook for another 2 minutes.

Tip the shallot mixture into the slow cooker pot with the beans, tomatoes, tomato vine, stock/broth, oregano and tomato purée/paste, then stir until combined, making sure the beans are covered by the liquid. Cover and cook for 2–3 hours on low or 1½–2 hours on high, until the beans are tender.

Spoon into a serving bowl, add the lemon juice and salt and pepper, to taste. Finish with a scattering of mint leaves.

CONFIT TOMATOES

The secret to the success of this recipe is choosing the best quality, vine-ripened, seasonal tomatoes you can – anything less will disappoint. Slow cooked until sweet and unctuous, the confit is delicious as a side dish, used in a sandwich or as a condiment. Cooking the tomatoes slowly at a low temperature in oil also greatly increases the body's ability to absorb the antioxidant lycopene.

400 g/14-oz. cherry tomatoes or small tomatoes on the vine, halved, vine saved
2 garlic cloves, thinly sliced
5 thyme sprigs
4 tbsp extra-virgin olive oil
1 tsp balsamic vinegar
sea salt and freshly ground black pepper

Low 1½–2 hours

Serves 4

Arrange the tomatoes in the base of the slow cooker pot in an even layer, you may have to overlap them in places. Arrange the slices of garlic in between the tomatoes, so they are evenly spread, and the thyme sprigs and reserved vine on top. Pour the olive oil and balsamic vinegar evenly over the top.

Cover and cook on low for 1½–2 hours, until the tomatoes soften and start to break down. Season with salt and pepper, to taste, and either spoon into a serving bowl or into a sterilised jar. Cover with the lid and store in the fridge for up to 2 weeks.

SLOW-SIMMERED COURGETTES/ZUCCHINI WITH GARLIC CRUMBS

Slow cookers are perfect for gently braising vegetables such as tomatoes, (bell) peppers, aubergine/eggplant and, as here, courgettes/zucchini. The courgettes/zucchini become meltingly soft, which works well with the contrast of the crisp garlic crumbs.

450 g/4½ cups courgettes/zucchini, cut into ½-cm/¼-in. thick rounds
2 garlic cloves, thinly sliced
3 tbsp extra-virgin olive oil
freshly squeezed juice of ½ lemon
sea salt and freshly ground black pepper

GARLIC CRUMBS
2 tbsp extra-virgin olive oil
90 g/1½ cups day-old fresh breadcrumbs
1 garlic clove, finely chopped
1 tsp finely grated lemon zest

Low 2–2½ hours
High 1½–2 hours

Serves 4

Put the courgettes/zucchini in the slow cooker pot with the sliced garlic and 3 tablespoons olive oil. Cover and cook for 2–2½ hours on low or 1½–2 hours on high, until the courgettes/zucchini are tender. Add the lemon juice and season with salt and pepper to taste.

Meanwhile, make the garlic crumbs. Heat the 2 tablespoons olive oil in a small frying pan/skillet over a medium heat, add the breadcrumbs and fry, stirring often, for 5 minutes, until light golden. Add the garlic and cook for another minute, stirring, taking care not to burn the garlic, until the crumbs are crisp. Remove from the heat and stir in the lemon zest, then leave to cool.

Transfer the courgettes/zucchini to a serving bowl and scatter over the garlic crumbs just before serving to prevent them turning soggy. Serve warm or at room temperature.

POTATO BOULANGERE

Layers of white and sweet potato are interspersed with sliced onions in a creamy, herby stock/broth, then topped with grated cheese to make a light meal for two with green veg or a side dish for four. The slightly tricky part of cooking this dish in a slow cooker is getting the creamy stock/broth levels just right, too much and the potato is swamped and too little and they won't cook. It also depends on how starchy your potatoes are.

30 g/2 tbsp butter or dairy-free alternative, plus extra for greasing

3 onions, thinly sliced

3 garlic cloves, thinly sliced

300 ml/1¼ cups hot vegetable stock/broth

5 tbsp double/heavy cream or dairy-free alternative

1 tbsp fresh thyme leaves

450 g/1 lb. white potatoes, such as Maris Piper, scrubbed and left unpeeled

450 g/1 lb. sweet potatoes, peeled

60 g/⅔ cup coarsely grated vegetarian Gruyère or Cheddar cheese or dairy-free alternative

sea salt and freshly ground black pepper

Low 4–5 hours
High 3–4 hours

Serves 2–4

Melt the butter in a large frying pan/skillet over a medium-low heat and sauté the onions for 8 minutes, until softened and starting to colour. Add the garlic and cook for another 2 minutes, stirring.

Meanwhile, pour the hot stock/broth into a jug/pitcher and stir in the cream and thyme. Season well with salt and pepper.

Lightly grease the slow cooker pot. Arrange half of the white potatoes in an even layer in the pot, then a third of the onion mixture, spreading it evenly. Top with half of the sweet potatoes and another third of the onion mixture. Pour over half of the creamy stock/broth mix. Finish off with another layer of white potato and onion and a final layer of sweet potatoes. Pour over the remaining creamy stock/broth and press the potatoes down into the stock/broth until as covered as possible.

Cover, lining the lid with kitchen paper/paper towels to absorb any moisture, and cook for 4–5 hours on low or 3–4 hours on high. One hour before the end of the cooking time, press the potatoes down into the creamy stock/broth to ensure they cook evenly, then scatter over the cheese. Replace the kitchen paper/paper towels if needed. Cover and continue to cook until the potatoes are tender when pierced with a skewer and the cheese has melted.

GARLICKY WHITE BEANS WITH LEMON

The simplest recipes are often the best and this couldn't be much easier – and healthy. You can use dried or canned beans for this dish, which can be served as part of a mezze-type meal – warm or at room temperature – or as a side dish.

2 x 400-g/14-oz. cans cannellini or butter/lima beans, drained and rinsed (or 200 g/1 cup dried cannellini, soaked overnight and cooked, drained (see page 14)

3 tbsp extra-virgin olive oil

2 large banana shallots, diced

1 celery stick/rib, finely chopped

1 garlic bulb, cut in half

250 g/8¾ oz. small vine-ripened tomatoes, halved

2 bay leaves

1 tsp vegetable bouillon powder

300 ml/1¼ cup just-boiled water

juice of ½ a lemon, freshly squeezed

1 large handful of chopped flat-leaf parsley

finely grated zest of 1 lemon

sea salt and freshly cracked black pepper

Low 4–5 hours
High 3–4 hours

Serves 4

Add the beans, olive oil, shallots, celery, garlic and tomatoes to the slow cooker pot and stir gently until combined. Tuck in the bay leaves.

Stir the bouillon powder into the hot water and pour it over the bean mixture. Cover and cook for 4–5 hours on low or 3–4 hours on high until the beans are tender. (If using cooked dried beans, cook for 6–7 hours on low and 5–6 hours on high, increasing the quantity of water to 400 ml/1¾ cups minus 1 tbsp and bouillon to 1½ tsp.) Stir in the lemon juice and season generously with salt and pepper.

Transfer the beans to a serving bowl and scatter over the parsley and lemon zest. Serve warm or at room temperature.

MASALA BAKED BEANS

A spicy twist on the classic beans in tomato sauce, this makes a good breakfast, cooked slowly overnight, or an any-time-of-the-day light meal. Nutritious, easy and economical, you could use dried beans instead of canned to cut costs further – you'll need about 150 g/5¼ oz. dried beans, then follow the instructions for cooking them on page 14. Rather than the usual toast, serve the beans on top of a warm naan.

1 tbsp coconut oil
1 onion, grated
400 g/14 oz. passata
1½ x 400-g/14-oz. can haricot beans, drained
1 tbsp tomato purée/paste
1 tsp raw apple cider vinegar
2 tsp coconut sugar, soft light brown sugar or molasses
½ tsp ground ginger
1 tsp garlic granules
1½ tsp curry powder
½ tsp ground turmeric
sea salt and freshly ground black pepper

TO SERVE
4 small naan breads, warmed
4 tbsp Coconut Raita
1 medium-hot green chilli/chile, deseeded and thinly sliced (optional)

COCONUT RAITA
100 ml/scant ½ cup coconut yogurt or live natural/plain yogurt
5-cm/2-in. piece of cucumber, quartered lengthways, seeds removed and finely diced
freshly squeezed juice of ½ small lemon
1 handful of chopped mint leaves
sea salt

Low 7–8 hours
High 3–4 hours

Serves 4

Heat the coconut oil in a frying pan/skillet over a medium heat. Add the onion and fry for 5 minutes, stirring, until softened.

Transfer the onion to the slow cooker pot with the passata, haricot beans, tomato purée/paste, vinegar and sugar or molasses and stir until combined. Cover and cook for 7–8 hours on low if you want to cook the beans overnight (you may need to add a splash of hot water towards the end of the cooking time if the sauce looks too dry) or for 3–4 hours on high. If cooking on high, add the passata to the frying pan/skillet with the fried onion to heat through before adding to the pot.

One hour before the end of the cooking time, stir in the ground ginger, garlic granules, curry powder and turmeric. Cover, lining the lid with kitchen paper/paper towels to absorb any moisture, and continue to cook until the beans are tender and the sauce has reduced and thickened. Season with salt and pepper to taste.

Serve the beans on top of a warm naan bread with a spoonful of raita and scattering of chilli/chile, if you like.

Coconut Raita: Mix together all the ingredients and season with salt.

FAVA BEAN DIP

Dried fava beans, also known as broad beans, produce an unbelievably smooth, creamy dip – they would also make a good alternative to chickpeas/garbanzo beans in homemade humous. Unlike the whole beans, the split variety don't require pre-soaking and cook more quickly, but are still a good source of protein and fibre/fiber. This also makes a good alternative to mash or an accompaniment to dishes such as roasted vegetables.

225 g/1⅓ cup split dried fava beans, rinsed
2 large garlic cloves, peeled and left whole
1 bay leaf
3 tbsp extra-virgin olive oil, plus extra for drizzling
juice of 1 lemon, freshly squeezed
sea salt and freshly cracked black pepper

CAPER TOPPING (OPTIONAL)
2 tbsp small capers, drained and patted dry
2 tbsp chopped flat-leaf parsley
¼ tsp dried chilli/hot pepper flakes

TO SERVE
vegetable crudités
tortilla chips

Low 2–3 hours
High 1½–2½ hours

Makes 6–8 servings

Put the fava beans in a saucepan and cover generously with just-boiled water from the kettle. Bring to the boil then boil the beans for 10 minutes, until starting to soften, skimming off any white froth that appears on the surface. Turn off the heat and tip the beans and cooking water into the slow cooker pot. Pour in extra just-boiled water, if needed, to cover the beans by about 5 cm/2 in. and add the garlic cloves and bay leaf. Cover and cook for 2–3 hours on low or 1½–2½ hours on high, until tender and starting to break down.

Drain the beans, saving the cooking water, and pick out the bay leaf. Put the beans and garlic in a blender or food processor with 2 tablespoons of the cooking water, the olive oil and lemon juice. Blend until smooth and creamy, then season generously with salt and pepper. Spoon into a serving dish.

Caper Topping: Mix together the capers, parsley and chilli/hot pepper flakes, then season with sea salt. Scatter the topping over the dip and finish with a good drizzle of olive oil.

BLACK LENTIL & OLIVE TAPENADE

Lentils are perhaps a slightly unusual addition to tapenade, the classic Provençal olive and caper spread, yet they are perfect for adding substance as well as boosting the protein, fibre, iron and B vitamin content. Depending on your preference, you can finely chop all the ingredients or briefly blend them in a mini food processor, which gives a smoother texture. You could also make a green version using green lentils and olives.

70 g/ ½ cup black beluga lentils, rinsed

45 g/½ cup minus 1 tbsp sun-dried tomatoes in oil, drained and finely chopped

300 ml/1¼ cups just-boiled water from the kettle

100 g/1 cup pitted black olives

2 garlic cloves

1 tbsp capers, drained and patted dry

freshly squeezed juice of ½ lemon

2 tbsp extra-virgin olive oil

large pinch of dried chilli/hot pepper flakes

2 handfuls of chopped flat-leaf parsley

sea salt and freshly ground black pepper

Low 4½–5½ hours
High 3½–4½ hours

Makes 8 servings

Put the lentils and sun-dried tomatoes in the slow cooker pot with the just-boiled hot water – it should just cover the lentils but not swamp them as you want to keep the water level as minimal as feasible to cook them. Cover and cook for 4½–5½ hours on low or 3½–4½ hours on high, until the lentils are tender. Add an extra tablespoon or two of hot water during the cooking if needed.

At this point you can either, roughly mash the cooked lentils and sun-dried tomatoes with the back of a fork, then tip them into a mixing bowl. Finely chop the olives, garlic, capers and add them to the bowl with the lemon juice, olive oil, chilli/hot pepper flakes and half the parsley. Season with salt and pepper, to taste, and mix gently until combined.

Alternatively, tip the cooked whole lentils and sun-dried tomatoes into a mini food processor with the olives, garlic and capers and blend very briefly to a coarse purée, adding a little lemon juice, if needed, to loosen. Stir in the lemon juice, olive oil, chilli/hot pepper flakes and half the parsley.

Spoon the tapenade into a serving bowl and scatter over the remaining parsley. The tapenade will keep for up to 3 days stored in an airtight container in the fridge.

AUBERGINE/EGGPLANT DIP

Rich and spicy, this aubergine/eggplant dip can be served as a side dish, as part of a mezze or as a main dish accompanied with your favourite grain. It comes with a range of health benefits, including antibacterial and antiviral properties thanks to the ginger, garlic, turmeric and chilli/chile.

2 tsp coriander seeds

2 tbsp extra-virgin olive oil

2 aubergines/eggplants, sliced into rounds and cut into small chunks

1 onion, grated

1 thumb-sized piece of fresh root ginger, grated

3 garlic cloves, finely chopped

½ tsp dried chilli/hot pepper flakes

1 tsp nigella seeds

1 tsp ground turmeric

1 tbsp tomato purée/paste

1 tsp honey or maple syrup

200 ml/¾ cup just-boiled water from the kettle

2 tbsp chopped coriander/cilantro leaves

1 tbsp chopped mint

sea salt and freshly ground black pepper

thick natural/plain yogurt or dairy-free alternative and flatbreads, to serve

Low 4–5 hours
High 3–4 hours

Makes 4 servings

Toast the coriander seeds in a large, dry frying pan/skillet over a medium-low heat for 2 minutes until they smell aromatic. Leave to cool then grind in a pestle and mortar or grinder.

Heat the olive oil in the frying pan/skillet, add the aubergines/eggplants and fry for 6 minutes, until starting to turn golden – it will look as though there's not enough oil at first, but persist and the aubergines/eggplants will start to release the oil as they cook. Stir in the onion, ginger and garlic and cook for another 5 minutes, until softened.

Stir in the coriander seeds and the rest of the spices, tomato purée/paste, honey or maple syrup and hot water. Cover and cook for 4–5 hours on low or 3–4 hours on high, until the aubergine/eggplant is very tender and the sauce has thickened, add a splash more hot water if needed.

Season with salt and pepper to taste and stir in the herbs. Spoon the relish into a bowl and serve topped with a spoonful of yogurt and flatbreads on the side.

RED CABBAGE WITH APPLE & CLOVES

The aroma of cloves and allspice, so reminiscent of Christmas, will fill your kitchen as the red cabbage slowly and gently simmers away. What's more, cooking the cabbage in a slow cooker frees up valuable hob space, a time when it is at a premium during the festive season. From a health perspective, red cabbage, like other brassicas, may protect against certain cancers and supports the health of the gut.

1 red onion, diced
475 g/8 cups red
    cabbage, shredded
2 dessert apples, cored
    and coarsely grated
    (no need to peel)
5 cloves
2 tbsp raw apple cider
    vinegar
freshly squeezed juice
    of 1 large orange
1 tsp light soft brown
    sugar
3 tbsp water
½ tsp ground allspice
sea salt and freshly
    ground black
    pepper

Low 4–5 hours
High 3–4 hours

Serves 4–6

Put all the ingredients up to and including the water in the slow cooker pot and mix until combined. Cover and cook for 4–5 hours on low or 3–4 hours on high.

One hour before the end of the cooking time, stir in the allspice and check the water levels, adding a splash more if the cabbage looks very dry. Season with salt and pepper, to taste, before serving.

SPICED BEETROOT/BEETS WITH DILL YOGURT

Beetroot/beets and orange are natural partners flavourwise, with the citrus curbing the earthiness of the vegetable. Both are a good source of vitamin C and other antioxidants.

1 tsp coriander seeds
400 g/3 cups uncooked beetroot/beets, peeled and cut into 2-cm/1-in. chunks
juice of 1 large orange
2 tsp raw apple cider vinegar
¼ tsp dried chilli/hot pepper flakes
sea salt and freshly ground black pepper

TO SERVE
200 g/1 cup thick natural/plain yogurt or dairy-free alternative
extra-virgin olive oil, for drizzling
1 large handful dill sprigs

Low 2–3 hours
High 1½–2 hours

Serves 4

Toast the coriander seeds in a small, dry frying pan/skillet over a medium-low heat for about 1 minute, until they smell aromatic. Tip into a pestle and mortar or mini grinder and grind to a powder.

Put the beetroot/beets in the slow cooker pot with the orange juice, vinegar, chilli/hot pepper flakes and ground coriander. Cover and cook for 2–3 hours on low or for 1½ –2 hours on high, until the beetroot/beets are tender. Season with salt and pepper to taste.

To serve, spoon the yogurt into a shallow serving dish and top with the beetroot and any juices in the pot. Finish with a drizzle of olive oil and a scattering of dill.

GREEN HERB & CHILLI SALSA

This salsa adds a pop of flavour and colour to soups, stews, roasts, stir-fries – almost anything really! You can vary the herbs and type of chilli/chile depending on what you are serving it with – mint and parsley or basil and coriander/cilantro are good herb blends, too.

1 large handful of chopped flat-leaf parsley (save the stalks for a soup or stew)

2 large handfuls of chopped coriander/cilantro leaves (save the stalks for a soup or stew)

1 medium-hot green chilli/chile, such as a jalapeño, finely chopped

1 small garlic clove, crushed

juice of ½–1 lemon, freshly squeezed

2 tbsp extra-virgin olive oil

sea salt and cracked black pepper

Makes 4–6 servings

Mix together all the ingredients in a serving bowl and season with salt and pepper to taste. Start with the smaller quantity of lemon juice, taste and add more, if needed. If you want a smoother salsa, put everything into a blender or mini food processor and briefly chop.

Serve straightaway or the salsa will keep for a day, stored in an airtight container in the fridge.

PICADA

Zesty, nutty and herby – this Spanish relish adds texture and a boost of flavour to vegetable and bean-based stews, grain and pasta dishes. It's traditionally pound to a paste, but I coarsely chop the almonds as I like it with a bit of crunch.

45 g/scant ½ cup almonds
1½ tbsp extra-virgin olive oil
65 g/2¼ oz. day-old bread, such as sourdough or ciabatta, crusts removed, cut into ½-cm/¼-in. cubes
1 small garlic clove, crushed

2 large handfuls of chopped flat-leaf parsley
finely grated zest of 1 unwaxed lemon
sea salt

Makes 4 servings

Toast the almonds in a large, dry frying pan/skillet over a medium-low heat for 5 minutes, turning once, or until starting to colour. Tip onto a chopping board and leave to cool.

Add 1 tablespoon olive oil to the pan/skillet and fry the bread for 5 minutes, turning occasionally, until golden and crisp. Stir the garlic into the pan and cook for another 30 seconds.

Coarsely chop the almonds, then add to a serving bowl with the parsley and lemon zest.

Roughly crush the bread with the end of a rolling pin and add to the bowl. Add a good pinch of salt and pour in the remaining oil. Stir until combined, then serve.

ALMOND AIOLI

Creamy and nutritious, add this vegan alternative to the egg-based classic to any dish that would benefit from a spoonful of mayonnaise.

150 g/1¼ cups blanched almonds
2 tbsp extra-virgin olive oil
2 garlic cloves
2 heaped tsp Dijon mustard
160 ml/⅔ cup almond milk or alternative
juice of 1 small lemon, freshly squeezed

sea salt and freshly cracked black pepper

Makes 4 servings

Toast the almonds in a large, dry frying pan/skillet over a medium-low heat for 5 minutes, turning once, or until starting to colour. Tip them into a bowl, cover with water and leave to soak for 1 hour.

Drain the almonds and put them in a food processor or blender with the oil, garlic, mustard, almond milk and lemon juice and blend until smooth and creamy. Season with salt and pepper, to taste, and add more lemon juice or milk if needed to make a mayonnaise-like consistency. The aioli will keep for up to 3 days stored in an airtight container in the fridge.

INDEX

ACKNOWLEDGMENTS

This book was such a delight to write. It came at a particularly stressful time in my life and I found the slow and methodical process of testing and writing incredibly grounding – almost therapeutic. Thank you once again Julia Charles, Editorial Director, for giving me the opportunity to publish another book with RPS; it has been such a pleasure. My thanks also go to Desk Editor Emily Calder for making the experience easy and seamless; to Creative Director Leslie Harrington for your excellent art direction as always; and to photographer and prop stylist, Kate Whitaker and food stylist Bianca Nice for making my recipes look so appetizing. Creating a book is always a team effort – heartfelt thanks to all!